The Dance

of the

Shulamite

By

Barbara Urban

The Dance of the Shulamite, by Barbara Urban
ISBN # 0-89228-148-0

Copyright ©, 2000 by Barbara Urban

Published by
Impact Christian Books, Inc.
332 Leffingwell Ave.,
Kirkwood, MO 63122
314-822-3309

Cover Design: *Ideations*

All Scripture references are taken from the *New King James Version*

Printed in the United States of America

Table of Contents

A Special Dedication

*This book is dedicated to all the handmaidens of the Lord who have been hidden in obscurity by the Lord's great jealousy over them. May you fulfill your destinies as **Daughters of Zion** whose garments have been washed in the **blood of the Lamb**. A few of these "daughters" of the King were instrumental in their spiritual and financial support of this book and its journey to publication. The world is not worthy of these for their "hiddenness" will soon reveal the wonder and beauty of their training in the kingdom for such a time as this. May Cathy Wills, Mollie Bowman, Pam Perlin, Charlene Stephenson, Neveda Wayland, and Barbara Long find grace to dance the great **Dance of the Shulamite** to the glory of the Beloved, Yeshua ha Meshiach. They are indeed His handmaidens, and I treasure their friendship to me as fellow handmaidens in His glorious kingdom. Dance, sisters, dance!*

The dance of the Shulamite...

is a dance of unbridled passion for the Son of God,

expressed in extravagant acts of unwavering obedience.

Introduction

We all have a dance in us. That dance is an expression of God within us, complimenting His kingdom. Unfortunately, many dance to the captivating sound of the prince and power of the air, while others are enslaved to the primal dance of their own carnality. Some even become ensnared by the dance of religion, chained to legalistic maneuvers which keep them far from the heart of the Father. But there are a few who actually hear the love call of the Beloved. They are the ones who break out of the confines of this life and live the life of the kingdom here and now, dispossessing powers and principalities by the very nature of their prophetic dance of passionate love and tenacious obedience. That is the Dance of the Shulamite.

This is a bridal dance of unparalleled devotion, allegorically depicted in the vivid portrait of the lavish love relationship between the "Shulamite" and the "Beloved" in Song of Songs. This is the dance of the Bride, and as such, it manifests itself as the most thrilling of dances, causing our lives to bring forth the very fruit for which they were created. But how do we know if we are dancing this spectacular Dance of the Shulamite? There are attributes that give it away, and only those who have sat under His apple tree, feasting upon His fruit, will discern that dance, and when they do, all other dances will be disdained.

Romanced

Under His

Apple Tree

Of Intimacy...

I. THE GLANCE THAT CAPTURES

Before one can dance the dance of the Shulamite, one's heart must be captivated by the glance of the Beloved....

My beloved is like a gazelle or a young stag.
Behold, he stands behind our wall;
He is looking through the windows,
Gazing through the lattice.

Song 2:9

All dances issue from the heart. As proclamations of who we are, they express our belief system and the unspoken priorities which we have embraced. Out of all the *dances* which we may dance in a lifetime, there is only one dance which is hidden within us by the predestination of God's plan for us. I like to refer to this special dance as the *dance of the Shulamite*.

This is a distinct dance, complimenting the kingdom of God and glorifying the Creator who created each of us to uniquely bear His image. Therefore, it is impossible to genuinely dance another's dance. You may imitate another person's dance, but you will only be playing out the inconsistencies and insecurities latent within your own heart.

To dance the *dance of the Shulamite* there must be a foundation of passion for the Son of God which has been ignited by the very *attentions* of the Son of God.

There can be no substitute. Our passion for the Beloved cannot be sustained by another person's passion for Him, otherwise we have fallen in love with the *mere idea* of being in love with God, and that is a cheap substitute for the real thing.

More important, the imitation of another person's passion for God can actually hinder the release of one's own life dance unto the Lord; and since artificial "passion" has to be continually fueled by the *artifices* of love, it cannot take the *reality* of love's embrace which **must** include *chastisement* to be a true expression of love. *"For whom the Lord loves He chastens, and scourges every son whom He receives"* *(Hebrews 12:6).*

God's chastisement enables us to grow and mature in our relationship with Him, but in order to bear such chastisement, it is imperative that we personally experience His transforming proclamations of love; for that is the basis of true passion for God. It is God's affirmations which capture our hearts, laying the foundation for relationship with Him. *"We love Him because He first loved us" (I John 4:19).* These *affirmations* are the essence of the *glance that captures*, and this *capturing* must be based on our individual interactions with Him as our **Redeemer *and* Spouse**. It is our relational development in these two areas which dictates the nature of the dance which will flow out of our lives.

Without embracing Christ as our Redeemer, we have no right to stand in His presence and enjoy His fellowship; and without an appreciation for our role as *His bride, His spouse,* the prophetic significance of our destiny is lost in a life of mere religious acts.

Our end truly is as His *bride,* and what that entails and how that gets expressed through our lives here on earth becomes our *dance.* If it is a dance of devotion out of a pure heart, cleansed by the Redeemer, it will evolve into the *dance of the Shulamite* because that is the dance of the Bride. **She dances a dance of unbridled passion, expressed by extravagant acts of unwavering obedience.**

This dance cannot be learned or choreographed; it is *birthed.* It is a dance specially reserved for those who venture beyond **the foundation of redemption** into *the mysterious realm of intimacy,* and the *fruit* of such intimacy with the Beloved is the birthing of this extraordinary dance.

It is in our quest for intimacy that we learn to hear the Beloved's voice, acquainting ourselves with His desires. As our commitment to Him and His ways

13

deepens, we begin to *obey* His voice out of devotion; and the *dance of the Shulamite* begins to come forth, bringing God glory and advancing His purposes.

This marvelous pursuit of intimacy is graciously initiated by the Beloved, and we have the choice of responding to Him or not. As our groom, He makes the advances; and as His bride, we choose how we will respond to His *passionate glances and elaborate gestures of love.*

Intriguingly, His *glance* is so powerful that it actually has the potential to hinder the flow of all other dances in our lives. It is His *glance* which awakens the latent seeds of holy passion within us, and as we perceive His *glance* and receive His affirmations, holy passions are stirred. If we attend to these stirrings, a flaming passionate love for the Son of God will be birthed, competing with all other dances in our lives. Thus, does the holy passion of the Shulamite for the Beloved ignite, and the love story of the ages moves forward, causing us to increasingly yearn for His attentions...

Let him kiss me with the kisses of his mouth—
For your love is better than wine.

Song 1:2

II.   RECLINING UNDER
HIS APPLE TREE...

To recline in the shade of His apple tree you must make your way to His secret garden...

Like an apple tree among the trees of the woods,
So is my beloved among the sons.
I sat down in his shadow with great delight,
And his fruit was sweet to my taste.

Song 2:3

Once you have let the Son kiss you with the *"kisses of His mouth" (Song 1:2),* the captivation of your heart has begun. This captivation is for the purposes of entering into the fullness of intimate relationship with God Himself. The fullness of what that relationship looks like is explored within His *secret garden.*

You may ask, where is His secret garden? Will I know when I am there? This special place is in the *shadow of His presence,* and He opens it up to those who diligently seek Him, desiring earnestly to know Him. We gain this desire when we respond to *His glance.*

As His glance captures our attention, our affections are enthralled by Him and His glorious beauty. We begin to fall in love with the Son for who He is—*the Beloved*—and not just for what He can do for us. It is in the capturing of our affections that we lay aside the other dances to which we have been captivated in the past and passionately pursue Him.

We discover that being in the Creator's presence is more than satisfying and extremely intoxicating, surpassing all other dances and vain pursuits. As such, our experiences with Him drive us to experience more of Him, and in our quest for Him we discover that He has more and more to show us. These revelations of Himself and His kingdom are the many fruits of His *apple tree.*

It is in the *shade of His apple tree* that we enjoy His words of love which possess the power to liberate us from the destructive lies of our past relationships with other *lovers.* These other lovers have included the pursuit of money, fame, position, power, possessions, relationships, ... and the list goes on. These vain pursuits have left many of us wounded and dissatisfied with life. In order to partake of *His fruit* we must allow Him to wean us off of this poison fruit from which we have been partaking.

His fruit satisfies, for it links us to our created destiny in Him. If we will allow His affirmations to displace the lies which we have formerly embraced, we will actually be liberated from our bondages and set free to live the life of the kingdom. That life comes forth as we turn away from our past dances and loves of this world and choose Him and Him alone.

His wooing of us is for the purpose of capturing not only our affections, but our *hearts* that we would love no other as we love Him. For He is our groom, and we are His bride; and as such, He *jealously* guards over our lives, desiring a single-eyed devotion from us. Given the fact that He has so lavishly displayed His unconditional love for us through His own sacrificial death on the cross, He deserves no less devotion from us.

Even though He has purchased us with His own blood, He will *wait* for us to *willingly* choose Him. It is by our own volitional choosing that we enter into a relationship of deep commitment and intimacy with Him. As He died to show His commitment to us, so He desires that we would *die* to our ways as an expression of our commitment to Him.

It is during our time under His apple tree that we are prepared for this level of commitment, for we find that we cannot live without Him, and to live with Him we must *obey* His mandates and comply with His demands. There is no other way to His heart, and to be a lover of God, we must find the way to *His heart.*

Our time under His apple tree is where we will be convinced of our need to *change* and comply with His demands. It is a place of reasoning between God and man, a place where we discover that *God's ways are not our ways.* It is under His apple tree that we begin to partake of life in Him. It is a place of discovery where the secrets of God and the secrets of our hearts are laid bare. It is a place of *intercourse* between God and man. Thus, is it a place of *fruitfulness*; for out of this *intercourse* comes the fruit of *change* and the transformation of us into His bride, a bride worthy of Him.

> *He brought me to the banqueting house.*
> *And his banner over me was love.*
> *Sustain me with cakes of raisins,*
> *Refresh me with apples,*
> *For I am lovesick.*
>
> *Song 2:4-5*

Chastened

By Love's Embrace

For His

Good Pleasure

III. FOLLOWING HIM
INTO THE WILDERNESS...

He grooms us for His purposes, and that grooming can involve a painful series of chastisements...in a desert place...in His chambers...

Draw me away!
We will run after you.
The king has brought me into his chambers.
Song 1:4a

It is at His banqueting table as He woos us with His fruits, causing us to be intoxicated with His delights, that He opens ours eyes and ears to *His desires,* revealing the inconsistencies within us which war against His purposes. He therefore entices us into His *chambers* for the purposes of *grooming and chastening* that we might come into the fullness of our inheritance as His sons and daughters. Without such chastisement, we are but illegitimate, losing any hope of a full inheritance in Him.

His chastisement actually changes us into His

image as His offspring, preparing us to take the land of our inheritance and dwell in it victoriously. It is the essence of our preparation as mighty warriors in His kingdom, and the success of this chastisement is dependent upon our *willingness* to sit at His feet in devotion, learning His ways that we might turn away from our ways; for it is in our growing adoration of Him that we repeatedly choose to lay down our lives for His purposes.

That is the call of the Bride—to *worship* Him and to *war* for His kingdom purposes which have been awakened within us through His divine interactions. That is the essence of the *dance of the Shulamite*, devoted obedience to the Master's every desire.

Without holy chastisement we will not be able to serve Him appropriately, for our best intentions will be but *religious zealotry*, fueled by the stench of self-righteousness. Chastisement exposes such impurities, declaring a need for a circumcision of the heart that our spirits might be set free to flourish in *His provision*.

It is in chastisement that we see our smallness and inadequacies, revealing the *counterfeit dances* to which we have been so tenaciously devoted in this life. The humiliation of such exposure manifests the greatness of His saving grace at work within us. Without such a revelation of His wondrous grace, we would never find His provision for us, and without His provision, we would never advance in His purposes for our lives.

It is through His chastening that we are *groomed* for His callings and purposes planted within us before the foundation of the world. *"For we are His workmanship, created in Christ Jesus for good works, which God prepared beforehand that we should walk in them" (Eph. 2:10).* This *grooming* causes us to be **overcomers**, revealing those bondages which keep us from fulfilling our divine imperatives, and then empowering us to *overcome* those bondages through His provision.

As God faithfully reveals the captivity to which we have been subject, He is also faithful to reveal His *strategies for war*, empowering us to overcome and enter into the occupation of our *promised land* in Him. Indeed, it is in the *wilderness* that the weapons of our warfare are realized, and it is to the degree that we embrace His *strategies for war* that we are actually schooled in the *mighty weaponry* of His kingdom. Therefore, it is our committed obedience to such *strategies* which dramatically releases the rich and unique choreography of the *war dance* of the Bride.

Our commitment to dancing the *war dance* of the Bride teaches us to feed upon **Him**—our **only** provision for deliverance. Without a committed expression of this *war dance* we will never enter into the *dance of the Shulamite*; for to enter into the true expression of this most sacred of dances, it is essential that we learn to feed upon Him. He is our *manna* from heaven, sent to feed us in the wilderness that we might pass *through* the wilderness and enter into our *inheritance* as His bride.

To learn to truly feast upon Him, He must lead us to a desert place where we have **no provision** of our own. It is then that both our need for Him and our resistance to Him are exposed. As the Lord delivered Israel from Egypt that He might lead her into the wilderness for the purposes of separating her unto Himself as His special treasure, teaching her to depend upon Him as her husband, so He desires to do the same with each of us who choose to follow Him there.

You have seen what I did to the Egyptians, and how I bore you on eagles' wings and brought you to Myself.

Now therefore, if you will indeed obey My voice and keep My covenant, then you shall be a special treasure to Me above all people; for all the earth is Mine.

Exodus 19:4-5

IV. FEASTING UPON THE BELOVED...

Feasting upon the Beloved is birthed in the wilderness, where our own provision has been stripped away...

I am the living bread which came down from heaven. If anyone eats of this bread, he will live forever; and the bread that I shall give is My flesh, which I shall give for the life of the world.

John 6:51

We will never feed upon Christ if we still have our own provision. To feed upon Him demands a level of faith to which the human will in its self-sufficiency is most resistant. Therefore, it is imperative that we be led to a place of *stripping*, for it is out of *necessity* that we learn to depend upon Him for our every need.

It is in our *neediness* that humility can be *birthed*, for godly humility is found in seeing ourselves the way God sees us, and He sees us as people in *need* of His provision. God's provision is welcomed through the *voice of humility*. Without humility we cannot even "see" the Lord's provision, much less take it, because our "seeing" His provision is dependent upon our self professed *need* for it. To actually "feed" upon that provision is an act of faith which can often *offend* our rationalizations and natural desires.

Jesus offended His followers by telling them, *"Most assuredly, I say to you, unless you eat the flesh of the Son of Man and drink His blood, you have no life in you" (John 6:53).* The reality of this statement will surely offend the most committed; for it is in the act of *trying* to feed upon Him that our deep-seated self-reliance and lack of faith in God and His mysterious ways are exposed.

It is in learning to feed upon His flesh that we learn to live by the Spirit. Indeed, His words to us are spiritual *manna* from heaven, and that manna is *life.* We must make a choice to follow His words which are *spirit*, turning away from the ways of this world which are but *flesh.* Our choice to pursue spirit *over* flesh is what propels us into His purposes, past the banality of life. But it is not an easy choice, for it involves the most spiritual of acts--*faith.* The writer of Hebrews reminds us that, *"[F]aith is the substance of things hoped for, the evidence of things not seen" (Hebrews 11:1).*

It is by faith that we access provision from the spiritual realm for the needs of the physical realm. It is in the spiritual realm of faith that the natural realm is made to bow to the greater reality of the spiritual realm. Yet, we cannot venture into a true walk of faith if our own provision still facilitates our lives, reducing faith to a mere concept with no power.

True faith is accessed out of our *need* for God to rescue us and do what He has promised. This *need* is realized in the wilderness where all natural provision is *gone*. It is there that our Master looms in the horizon of our lives as our great and mighty Warrior King, causing us to declare with the Shulamite,

> *Who is this coming out of the wilderness*
> *Like pillars of smoke,*
> *Perfumed with myrrh and frankincense,*
> *With all the merchant's fragrant powders?*
> *Song 3:6-8*

It is when we begin to behold our Redeemer out of our desperate *need* that we begin to know Him as our *Provider* and *Deliverer;* and that provision and deliverance is dependent upon our own obedient walk of faith as we feast upon His every word to us. As we actively choose to turn away from the ways of this world and its defiled provision, we begin to *feast on Him.* Of such, Jesus said, *"He who eats My flesh and drinks My blood abides in Me, and I in him" (John 6:56).*

To eat of Him in this fashion can and does involve a direct confrontation with the natural realm and its testimony. That is why faith is necessary. Without faith His provision cannot be accessed; for it is spiritual food that has the potential to impact and *change* the natural realm.

Invading the natural realm with provision from the spiritual realm often involves a series of *contradictions*. These contradictions are the *spasms* of the physical realm resisting the edicts of the spiritual realm, thereby testing the declarations of faith concerning God's kingdom. It is for those who *endure* such contradictions, professing faith in God's words of life to them in the face of such seeming obstacles, that provision comes. It is when you enter into *that* provision that you are *feeding* upon Him and therefore *abiding* in Him.

That place of *abiding* is a most coveted place of *rest*, and it is the ***only*** environment where the *dance of the Shulamite* blooms as the devoted dance of the Bride for the Beloved. Truly, this is a spiritual dance to which we are called to dance, and its life is fueled by ***faith*** in God's words to us; therefore, it is only attained as we learn to *obey* His words and live upon the promises He has spoken to us as spiritual *manna*; for they are truly ***"Yes" and "Amen."***

> *For all the promises of God in Him are Yes, and in Him Amen, to the glory of God through us.*
> *II Corinthians 1:20*

28

V. DRINKING OF HIM...

The life is in the blood, and the life behind the dance of the Shulamite is in Christ's blood...

For the life of the flesh is in the blood, and I have given it to you upon the altar to make atonement for your souls; for it is the blood that makes atonement for the soul.

Leviticus 17:11

Foundational to the *dance of the Shulamite* is learning not only to feast upon His every word, but to "drink" His blood that His life might flow through us. The first impartation of that life happens when we accept His redemptive work on the cross, allowing our spirits to be born anew. Because the life of Christ's blood is eternal, it has the power to bring life out of death which is what redemption is all about; however, there is a "drinking" of His blood which must happen daily for His redemption in us to have its *perfect work.* That "drinking" comes through a growing revelation and application of His blood to our lives.

His blood not only has the power to cleanse us

from sin, but it has a *voice* which has the power and authority to *silence* all other voices railing against us and God's purposes for our lives. His voice beckons to us at every level of maturity in the kingdom, declaring the purposes of God throughout the creation—*His wondrous redemption.* If we actually *hear* its mighty proclamations with a *kingdom understanding*, we can be empowered by them, joining our voices with them in faith.

> *But you have come to Mount Zion and to the city of the living God, the heavenly Jerusalem, to an innumerable company of angels, to the general assembly and church of the firstborn who are registered in heaven, to God the Judge of all, to the spirits of just men made perfect, to Jesus the Mediator of the new covenant, and to the blood of sprinkling that speaks of better things than that of Abel.*
>
> *Hebrews 12:22-24*

This blood speaks of "better things," declaring the powerful redemption of God available to all who seek Him. The speaking voice of the blood is a voice of triumph over our enemies, for it proclaims the complete and utter destruction of demonic powers and principalities which Christ made an open display of on the cross. *"Having disarmed principalities and powers, He made a public spectacle of them, triumphing over them in it" (Colossians 2:15).* In fact, Christ's blood aggressively declares the ***absolute*** destruction of God's foe, the devil. *"Inasmuch then as the children have partaken of flesh and blood, He Himself likewise shared in the same that through death He might destroy him who had the power of death, that is, the devil" (Hebrews 2:14).*

As we learn the power of Christ's finished work on the cross and what that means to us in our struggle over sin, we will obtain the victory, for the blood ever speaks on our behalf. However, it is by *faith* that we release its powerful voice. This truth which the blood speaks is unleashed only to the degree that we stand in it by *faith*, declaring it over our lives and choosing to turn away from the lies of the evil one.

By choosing to *hear* the blood, living by its life-giving pronouncements, the other voices in our lives are systematically silenced; for the blood silences them, literally warring on our behalf. The blood is ever faithful to declare us not guilty when the other voices in our lives condemn us, but we must release its voice by *faith*, not drawing back in unbelief; for *there is no other sacrifice that can be made.* It is therefore imperative that His life blood be appropriated to every area of our lives, as it is our *only* provision for coming in closer to the Beloved.

As the priests under the Old Covenant were diligent to sacrifice and cover specific sins with the blood of animals, so we too must be diligent with the blood of Christ, using it to silence every voice of

31

accusation against us. The blood ever speaks, but we must *appropriate* it and believe its testimony, or we will continue to live under the bondage of our own personal *Egypt*.

The blood is our complete provision for walking out from under the bondage of Egypt and its way of thinking that we might embrace the ways of the kingdom. This involves a renewing of our minds into which the testimony of the blood can consistently and effectively walk us.

> *And do not be conformed to this world, but*
> *be transformed by the renewing of your mind,*
> *that you may prove what is that good and*
> *acceptable and perfect will of God.*
> *Romans 12:2*

We must so embrace the testimony of the blood that the realities of the physical realm are dwarfed in comparison; for His blood is sufficient. It is our absolute and final victory over sin and death—past, present, and future. As we learn to "drink" of this blood which ever speaks, the reality of its victory over sin and death will subjugate our spiritual enemies, causing the natural realm to bow to the spiritual realm. This *subjugation* is quite literally accomplished as we choose to believe the voice of the blood of Christ over all the other voices which we hear.

The "drinking" of the truth of the power of Christ's blood causes His blood to mingle with our blood, beginning a mighty deliverance from the darkness that has bound us; therefore, silencing the voices of those strongholds with the reality of Christ's ultimate victory over powers and principalities. As this deliverance evolves and we stand by faith on more and more of God's truth, the voice of the blood becomes louder in our lives, causing the anointing of God to intensify as God's very presence increasingly rests upon us.

As our source of deliverance, we must let the blood's voice war for us, learning to rally by faith behind its mighty cry. Then will our enemies indeed bow at our feet. What else can they do? They cannot rail against the truth of the blood. The blood speaks of their total *defeat.*

Because the blood has the power to deliver us from our bondages, it also has the power to gird us up for war against our enemies; for it is the *voice of His blood* which leads us into war and victoriously out of war. This girding up for war is the *authority* that the blood brings to our lives in Christ Jesus; consequently, *the speaking voice of the blood is our empowerment for triumph over our enemies and for the exploits to which we have been called to do in Christ Jesus.* Therefore, a revelation of Christ's blood and its power to speak on our behalf is essential in our struggle over sin and death and in the realization of our purposes and callings which have been assigned to us in the kingdom.

The blood of Christ Jesus is unequivocally the lethal weapon which destroys our enemies. It has the last word on all spiritual debates, and no testimony can stand against its voice when it has been activated by the proclamation of faith spoken by those who rally behind it.

As we partake of the blood as provision for living an overcoming life, victorious over our enemies, His life of sacrifice and servanthood is imparted, calling us to walk in His ways. As such, we may hear Him asking us to do things we would never choose to do with our carnal minds. Consequently, the blood literally leads us into the paths of righteousness for Christ's name sake that His kingdom might go forth.

Such is the life force of the blood; it imparts the very heart of God to us, causing us to desire to follow Him as His devoted servants, wherever He leads. That is the mark of a true imbiber of Christ—one who knows God's heart and walks to His heartbeat, fulfilling His desires. That is the essence of an *overcomer*; someone who has overcome his own fear and self-centeredness by the impartation of life from the speaking voice of the blood of the Lamb, partaking of Christ's very nature. Therefore, is death ever so dramatically swallowed up in victory as we choose to die to our desires and live to His; for it is in losing our lives that we find them. *"For whoever desires to save his life will lose it, but whoever loses his life for My sake will find it" (Matthew 16:25).*

Our imbibing of Christ's spiritual life blood causes its redemptive life force to flow through our veins, instigating the redemption of our bodies, souls, and spirits, calling us out from a life of carnality and death. Once we begin the process of *drinking* this powerful blood which imparts redemption and life to us, we are pushed and pulled into a series of situations and circumstances that cause us to be conformed into His image; for it is in the repeated trials of our life that we are given the opportunity to loose the speaking voice of the blood upon our spiritual enemies, teaching us to not only walk by the Spirit, but also to *war* by the Spirit. It is indeed the walking out of our daily warfare that transforms us into *overcomers,* overcomers who bear His image and *follow the Lamb wherever He leads.*

Through our simple proclamations of faith in God's complete provision for redemption, standing on what God has said and done, and declaring them unwaveringly to the spirit realm, a spiritual shift in power is accomplished. A *violence* erupts out of this type of faith which causes powers and principalities to be dramatically dispossessed by our very proclamations and acts of obedience to the Son. When the proclamation of the blood has become *our proclamation,* a mighty stir in the heavens will surely ensue; for it is the proclamation of *life*—life eternal.

Our testimony as overcomers will evolve out of our unwavering belief in the power of Christ's atoning blood. As we grow in our revelation of the blood's voice, our testimony will indeed become faithful and true, echoing the testimony of our Redeemer.

This is one of the mighty weapons in the King's arsenal—*His blood*. His own sacrifice has secured victory for His people, and as His blood speaks on our behalf, we will walk as overcomers, joining our voices to that voice; for it is an *overcoming voice... a voice of victory... a voice of redemption... a voice of **life**.* Those who hear and live by this voice will indeed be overcomers, the very ones of whom it will be said, *"And they overcame him by the blood of the Lamb and by the word of their testimony, and they did not love their lives to the death" (Revelation 12:11).*

It is up to us to walk in the victory that has been purchased for us. Such a victorious walk as this comes at the consequence of much violence in the spirit realm; for vain imaginations and false perceptions must be violently cast down and made to bow to the testimony of Jesus. *"And from the days of John the Baptist until now the kingdom of heaven suffers violence, and the violent take it by force" (Matthew 11:12).*

As the children of Israel were called to judge those who occupied their land of promise by utterly destroying them, so are we. Each of us has a prophetic land of promise which looms in the horizon; and to ascend to it, we will need to fight. And to win, we will need to learn to wield the weapons of our warfare.

For the weapons of our warfare are not carnal but mighty in God for pulling down strongholds, casting down arguments and every high thing that exalts itself against the knowledge of God, bringing every thought into captivity to the obedience of Christ, and being ready to punish all disobedience when your obedience is fulfilled.

II Corinthians 10: 4-6

When we allow the Lord's judgments to have their perfect work in us *first*, literally chasing out the darkness that has reigned within us, we position ourselves to *fulfill our obedience* unto Him. Such obedience to the mandates of the kingdom causes the voice of the darkness which once reigned in us to be brought into subjection to the overpowering voice of the blood of the Lamb. As we are faithful to do this, the blood victoriously announces the kingdom of our God and the destruction of the enemy's kingdom. That is the essence of our *dance of war* unto the Groom, releasing His blood to silence the lying, condemning voices of the kingdom of darkness. As the enemy is dispossessed from our lives, the kingdom of God advances and His anointing increases upon the earth.

The *dance of the Shulamite* is just such an

overcoming dance of victory, proclaiming the victory which Christ Himself has accomplished through His death and resurrection, empowering us to be victorious in the midst of the troubled situations of our lives. In order to dance this dance fully, it is imperative that we come to a heightened practical revelation of the *blood of the Lamb*; for it is out of such revelation that we are liberated to truly dance this wondrous dance of victory with unrestrained abandon, *loving not our lives to the death.*

> *He who overcomes shall inherit all things, and I will be his God and he shall be My son.*
>
> *Revelation 21:7*

VI.   SOAKING IN HIS SPICES...

The wilderness is a place of tremendous change...
where our garden becomes His garden.

> *My beloved has gone to his garden,*
> *To the beds of spices,*
> *To feed his flock in the gardens,*
> *And to gather lilies.*
> *I am my beloved's,*
> *And my beloved is mine.*
> *He feeds his flock among the lilies.*
>   *Song 6:2-3*

It is in the *wilderness* that the Beloved begins to transform us into His bride that He might be equally yoked. As He teaches us to eat and drink of Him, we are transformed into a *garden enclosed*, consecrated for His purposes. *"A garden enclosed is my sister, my spouse, a spring shut up, a fountain sealed" (Song 4:12)*. No longer are we a *garden unto ourselves*; for as we willingly give up ownership, we become a garden unto Him, a precious treasure for *His enjoyment*.

It is in the wilderness through a series of well choreographed "deaths" that the *dance of the Shulamite* is crafted, evolving into a *dance of consecration* as we faithfully sanctify our lives and our ways to the enjoyment of the Beloved and Him alone. This consecration is orchestrated by the Beloved Himself, for it is He who has made provision for us that we might be perfected and made worthy of His purposes.

Just as Esther was *soaked* in specific spices within the palace to prepare her for her presentation before the king *(Esther 2:12)*, so are we *soaked* in special spices, causing us to emanate the very fragrances of His kingdom. The Lord desires to join Himself with a bride who emits such an intoxicating aroma; consequently, He soaks us in His Holy Spirit, filling us and baptizing us into His purposes that this *kingdom fragrance* might come forth.

The primary call of the Bride is to please the Bridegroom; therefore, does the Beloved woo us out into the wilderness that He might further prepare us for His purposes, circumcising our flesh and soaking us in the perfumes of His Holy Spirit that we might be a pleasing fragrance unto Him; for we were made for His good pleasure. Hosea picturesquely prophesied this divine purpose of God in dealing with His bride.

> *"Therefore, behold, I will allure her,*
> *Will bring her into the wilderness,*

40

And speak comfort to her.
I will give her her vineyards from there,
And the Valley of Achor as a door of hope;
She shall sing there, as in the days of her youth,
As in the day when she came up from the land of
Egypt.
And it shall be, in that day," Says the Lord,
"That you will call Me 'My Husband,'
And no longer call Me 'My Master,'
For I will take from her mouth the names of the
Baals,
And they shall be remembered by their name no
more."

Hosea 2:14-17

This dramatic transformation is wrought in the wilderness of our lives and accomplished through the testings of our faith as He grooms us to believe His words over the lies of the enemy. It is then that we are able to choose Him even in the face of glaring trials and heartbreaking tribulations. In fact, He brings us to a place of repeatedly choosing Him in the face of such trials because He has captivated us with His *glance*, causing us to cease the foolish dances we have been dancing. It is out of such testing that we begin to dance the dance of single-eyed devotion, the *dance of the Shulamite*.

When our commitment to Him causes us to weather the trials of life with unwavering faith in His provision, boldly challenging the contradictions of the natural realm, then does an *aroma* rise up from our lives. That aroma is released as we die to our ways and our provision, allowing His ways to envelop us. In this fashion are the "names of the Baals" removed from our lips that we might be a chaste bride worthy of His affections.

When His name is the *only* name on our lips, we carry *His scent*, the scent of a sacrificial life, representing our great Kinsman- Redeemer to the world. *"For we are to God the fragrance of Christ among those who are being saved and among those who are perishing" (II Corinthians 2:16)*. It is the obedient expression of our love for Him that releases the fragrance of His name as an *ointment* to a dying world.

> *Because of the fragrance of your good ointments,*
> *Your name is ointment poured forth;*
> *Therefore the virgins love you.*
> *Song 1:3*

As Christ gave Himself for us *"...an offering and a sacrifice to God for a sweet-smelling aroma" (Ephesians 5:2b)*, so, too, are we called to follow after Him and give ourselves to His purposes that His aroma might spring forth from us to His good pleasure. The Lord truly delights in the *death* of His saints, because it is in our *death to self* that His life, hidden within us, is released. *"Precious in the sight of the Lord is the death of His saints" (Psalm 116:15)*.

Thus is the wilderness a necessary time of preparation for the Bride to make herself ready for the Groom. It is a time of death to self and a time of soaking in His spices that we might be pleasing to Him. As His bride, captured by His glance and enraptured by His affections toward us, *His pleasure becomes our consuming passion.* Therefore are we destined to declare the cry of the Shulamite, *"I am my beloved's and my beloved is mine..." (Song 6:3).*

When our garden truly becomes His garden, then the winds of life which blow upon our garden, whether they be harsh winter winds of affliction or warm gentle breezes of refreshing, will consistently emit *His fragrance.* Because of a deepened revelation of the Beloved's pleasure in smelling that fragrance, we will begin to *embrace* tribulation, proclaiming with the Shulamite,

> *Awake, O north wind,*
> *And come, O south!*
> *Blow upon my garden,*
> *That its spices may flow out.*
> *Let my beloved come to his garden*
> *And eat its pleasant fruits.*
>
> *Song 4:16*

That is the beauty of the Bride, that she would cease to merely *react* to the trials of life, tossed to and fro like a wave of the sea, but instead would choose to live life out of a higher revelation gained by sitting at the Beloved's feet in pure devotion, *responding* in faith to life's struggles. It is at His feet that the bondages of this life lose their hold, and the revelations of His kingdom capture us, holding us entranced by Him and His glorious beauty. When the Bride lives life on this level, she will emit the fragrance of her lover, Christ Jesus.

As we commit ourselves to Him as His *bond slave*, sitting at His feet and living upon His every word, He is able to complete His transformation of us into His bride, and that mysterious transformation will necessarily involve a *baptism in myrrh* as we are taken deeper into His ways, joined to Him as His partner. This "baptism" leads us to actually *embrace suffering*. To engage in this level of service for our Lord, we will need a revelation of *His sufferings*, for He does indeed call us to drink *His cup* in the dark night of the soul that our companionship with Him might deepen; therefore, does He come to us, wooing us to join Him in the "night" of our lives.

> *I sleep, but my heart is awake;*
> *It is the voice of my beloved!*
> *He knocks, saying,*
> *"Open for me my sister, my love,*
> *My dove, my perfect one;*
> *For my head is covered with dew,*
> *My locks with the drops of the night."*
> *Song 5:2*

VII. THE BAPTISM OF MYRRH

There is a baptism into His sufferings, an anointing of myrrh, which joins the Bride to the very purposes of the Groom.

> *I arose to open for my beloved,*
> *And my hands dripped with myrrh,*
> *My fingers with liquid myrrh,*
> *On the handles of the lock.*
>
> *Song 5:5*

Dying to self in the wilderness, the Bride comes to increased revelations of true *servanthood*. It is here that we discover that *suffering* is more than something we bear, but something we can *embrace*; for it is a doorway into His deeper purposes for us as His bride. Indeed, it is in our *sufferings* for righteousness' sake that we are joined with Him more fully, bearing the marks of our groom, the Lord Jesus. *"For to you it has been granted on behalf of Christ, not only to believe in Him, but also to suffer for His sake" (Philippians 1:29).*

Suffering marks us as those *who follow the Lamb wherever He leads (Rev. 14:4), loving not our lives to* *the death (Rev. 12:11).* By *embracing* our sufferings, we manifest the reality that we are not of this world. Indeed, we possess a purpose beyond the banal trials of the natural realm; and the degree to which we embrace these *trials* causes us to enter into the realm of the *overcomer.*

The *overcomer* has risen above the limitations of the natural realm, dispossessing powers and principalities through a *tenacious obedience* to the desires of the Groom. Though His desires can be demanding, often causing us to *die* progressive deaths within our self-life, they potentially release the intoxicating *aroma* of the Spirit who lives within us. Thus are we adjured to sit at *His table* that we might actually enter into His sufferings, and therefore, exude *His life* to the world around us.

> *While the king is at his table,*
> *My spikenard sends forth its fragrance.*
> *A bundle of myrrh is my beloved to me,*
> *That lies all night between my breasts.*
> *My beloved is to me a cluster of henna blooms*
> *In the vineyards of En Gedi.*
>
> *Song 1:12-14*

As we suffer for the purposes of the kingdom, we demonstrate to the spirit realm that we actually *believe* what the Lord has said about Himself and us.

*If you were of the world, the world would love its own.
Yet because you are not of the world, but I chose you
out of the world, therefore the world hates you.
Remember the word that I said to you, "A servant is
not greater than his master." If they persecuted Me,
they will also persecute you...*

John 15:19-20

The essence of the Beloved as a suffering servant
is captured in *Song 4:6: "Until the day breaks and the
shadows flee away, I will go my way to the mountain of
myrrh and to the hill of frankincense."* This is a
dramatic picture of suffering not for sufferings' sake,
but for the purposes of the kingdom, as Christ did in
Gethsemane and on the cross of Calvary. The Beloved
came to suffer and die that He might redeem a people
whom He would call His pure and spotless bride. It is
through such strategic sufferings on His part that our
righteousness was secured, allowing Him to
prophetically say of His bride, *"You are all fair, my
love, and there is no spot in you" (Song 4:7).*

As His bride and servants of His kingdom, we, too,
are called to suffer for strategic purposes, purposes that
will dramatically advance the kingdom of God if we
would only embrace them.

*For it was fitting for Him, for whom are all things and
by whom are all things, in bringing many sons to
glory, to make the captain of their salvation perfect*

47

through sufferings.

For both He who sanctifies and those who are being sanctified are all of one, for which reason He is not ashamed to call them brethren, saying: "I will declare Your name to My brethren; In the midst of the assembly I will sing praise to You."

Hebrews 2:10-12

It is as we begin to walk in this truth, laying our lives down *daily* for His kingdom, obeying Him with eyes full of faith, and feeding on His provision that we take our seat in the heavenlies. As we dare to step into these *divine ordeals*, bearing the testings of the physical realm which beat upon us, we prove that our *revelation* of the kingdom has indeed transported us to heavenly places. Thus are powers and principalities *dispossessed*, allowing us to take our rightful place next to our Lord at His throne as His bride.

This dramatic and wondrous transformation is all accomplished by faith in *His provision*, not our provision; and His provision for dispossessing powers and principalities is found in *His body and His blood*. To feast upon these involves a radical transformation of our minds as we move from a base of *carnality*, to one of *spirituality*, putting on the mind of Christ to the glory of God the Father. This is all accomplished through the complete provision of the Son. He is our *meat and our drink*, our very sustenance for living and abiding in heavenly places with Him.

As we learn to *abide* in Him, we take our place at His side in heavenly places, judging the powers of darkness through our avid obedience to His divine strategies. This is the call of the Bride. She is prophetically called to dance this spectacular dance of *obedience,* overcoming the enemy of her soul through *the blood of the Lamb and by the word of her testimony, loving not her life unto the death (Revelation 12:11),* thereby disarming the powers of the evil one through the weapons of her warfare which are *"not carnal, but mighty in God for pulling down strongholds" (II Corinthians 10:4).*

This is the essence of the *dance of the Shulamite,* a mighty dance of war which erupts out of a deep affection for the Beloved, Christ Jesus. When we begin to walk by faith in the truths of God bestowed upon us through the atonement, we put on the weapons of our warfare, allowing Him to spiritually *clothe* us in *His authority.* That authority is a prophetic proclamation of who *He is,* announcing His sovereignty to the spirit realm. As His bride, clothed in this authority, we appear as a mighty army, waving these banners of truth, declaring His rule over the earth. Thus does the Bride become an awesome army of ravishing delight to the Groom, causing Him to proclaim,

> *O my love, you are as beautiful as Tirzah,*
> *Lovely as Jerusalem,*
> *Awesome as an army with banners!*
> *Turn your eyes away from me,*

For they have overcome me.

What is so ravishing about this spectacular sight that God, being *overcome*, would ask His bride to turn away? It is the sight of a Bride who has been prepared to rule and reign with Him throughout eternity. This Bride, prepared by the Holy Spirit to be a helpmate to the Groom, will bear the very mark of the Beloved, causing her to be that ravishing sight that overcomes Him.

The Father destined that His Son would be equally yoked to a bride worthy of His Son. As such, the Son's bride had to be purchased by the Son's own blood, causing her to look and smell like the Son. When the Bride begins to actually manifest the fullness of what has been prophetically deposited within her, she will *overcome* Her Beloved, winning His heart; for she will bear *His mark*, clothed in *His own righteousness* and redeemed by *His own blood,* the blood of the great and mighty Kinsman-Redeemer. The captivating glance of such single-eyed devotion coming from this stunning bride will cause the Creator of the universe to be overcome by the mere sight of her; for her beauty will be His own, and since she bears His beauty, she will bear His traits, carrying them as *banners of truth.*

You have ravished my heart,
My sister, my spouse;
You have ravished my heart

With one look of your eyes,
With one link of your necklace.
How fair is your love,
My sister, my spouse!
How much better than wine is your love,
And the scent of your perfumes
Than all spices!
Your lips, O my spouse,
Drip as the honeycomb;
Honey and milk are under your tongue;
And the fragrance of your garments
Is like the fragrance of Lebanon.

Song 4:9-11

Groomed

To Worship

and

To War

VIII. AWESOME AS AN ARMY WITH BANNERS

The Bride's faith in the Groom's provision arrays her in the very perfumes of the Beloved Himself, transforming her into ... an army with banners.

Who is she who looks forth as the morning,
Fair as the moon,
Clear as the sun,
Awesome as an army with banners?
                                        Song 6:10

It is during our time in the wilderness that we discover that the Bride's prophetic dance is not just a dance of *devotion*, but one of *war* as well. As such, we discover that we have been drafted into the Groom's *army*, and that army is "an army with banners," actually *ravishing* the very heart of our God.

To be transformed into that prophetic *army with banners*, we must have revelation of what those banners are which we have been called to rally around. In the desert times, we encounter those "banners" as *characteristics* of God in which we can trust and depend. As such, they empower us to overcome life's obstacles, causing us to be an *army of overcomers*, dancing to the truth of those banners.

To acquaint us with such banners of truth, God has to take us to a desert place where our provision is *gone*, so that He can reveal the many aspects of *His provision*. He cannot reveal Himself as our Provider if we have no need of provision. It is the revelation of our *neediness* that causes us to see Him as He truly is, and His attributes become life to us.

As we come to increased revelation of specific characteristics concerning God, those attributes become *banners of hope* to which we can run for all of life's needs. As such, our increased faith in such aspects of God's character causes us to boldly do exploits for His kingdom. Thus, do we literally push back the powers of darkness as we look to God's attributes as *banners of refuge* and proclaim in faith what God can be trusted to do for us.

This is the basis of our warfare, merely *believing* God and *resting* in His indisputable traits. It is our faith in who God is which releases Him to *do* what He said He would do. Consequently, it is our *dependence* upon God which causes the darkness to flee, for God responds to our *faith* and does what is true to His nature. *He can do no less.* Thus does the writer of Hebrews tell us, *"But without faith it is impossible to please Him, for he who comes to God must believe that He is, and that He is a rewarder of those who diligently seek Him" (Hebrews 11:6).*

Our faith moves God, for it is our faith in Him and His provision which causes us to appear as an *army with many banners,* and He is ravished by that. ***He is literally ravished by our faith.*** His delight in our unwavering faith overwhelms Him so intensely that at the captivating sight of His bride who abides in Him by faith, He must say to her, *"Turn your eyes away from me, for they have overcome me" (Song 6:5).*

If you have ever wanted to touch the heart of God, the key is simply having *faith in who God says He is.* Sincere faith in God and His characteristics moves the heart of God more deeply than we know. That type of faith not only moves God's heart, but according to *Matthew 17:20,* it moves mountains which stand in the way of our purposes in the kingdom; *"...I say to you, if you have faith as a mustard seed, you will say to this mountain, 'Move from here to there,' and it will move; and nothing will be impossible for you."* The enemy must flee when we learn to believe God, for God Himself arises and moves on our behalf.

The manifestation of this coveted type of faith is not the *presumptuous* proclamations of many to which we have been exposed. True faith in God is birthed in the wilderness of our lives when our desperation for God and His ways drives us to the Lord's banqueting table, seeking His provision for our need, causing us to *eat His flesh and drink His blood.* It is in our Lord's spiritual *body and blood* that we find provision to accomplish the mighty acts of faith to which we have been called.

This phenomenal faith of which we speak is actually birthed out of *death*—death to self and self-reliance. As such, it is truly in the desert that our eye is *captured* by the sight of our Beloved coming up out of the desert arrayed in His kingly splendor, sending our enemies to flight. For it is in our *desperation* that the deception of self-reliance is exposed as futile and useless, liberating us to actually *see* the Beloved as our great Deliverer rising up in our defense.

The wilderness is God's great equalizer, and as such it allows each of us the opportunity to see our *deficiency* and *His might.* It is in that revelation that we must choose to die to our meager provision that He might feed us, for without His intervention, we would surely die in the wilderness. When our eyes are opened, and we feast upon Him as our great Deliverer, our prophetic cry will profoundly and insightfully join with that of the Shulamite,

> *Who is this coming out of the wilderness*
> *Like pillars of smoke,*
> *Perfumed with myrrh and frankincense,*
> *With all the merchant's fragrant powders?*

Behold, it is Solomon's couch,
With sixty valiant men around it,
Of the valiant of Israel.
They all hold swords,
Being expert in war.
Every man has his sword on his thigh
Because of fear in the night.

Song 3:6-8

The real revelation in seeing our Beloved arising to do battle, coming out of the desert as a *pillar of smoke*, is that *we* are the valiant men beside Him, *expert in war*. To the degree that we embrace and stand in this truth will we become empowered to *chase* our enemies, knowing that it is the Beloved, Christ Jesus, who leads us into battle. It is His desire that we would destroy our enemies who stand in the way of His purposes. *Leviticus 26:7* declares to the obedient, *"You will chase your enemies, and they shall fall by the sword before you."*

To be successful in this warfare to which He calls us, we must find our way to His chambers. *Solomon's couch* communicates a prophetic picture of Christ's bridal chamber, a key in waging successful war for His kingdom. It is as we come into intimacy with the Beloved, abiding in Him, that we are empowered to war with Him. It is our abiding in Him, rallying behind His banners of truth which empowers us for battle. Indeed, the essence of our warfare is to *rest in Him*, feeding upon His words to us and obeying Him. For our war truly is *His war*, and He is the Warrior King. As we come to abide in that revelation, we find a most coveted place of rest and victory in Him. ***We find a place of peace in the midst of war.*** *"Then I became in his eyes as one who found peace" (Song 8:10b).*

Interestingly, the name *"Shulamite"* means *"peace"* as does the name *"Solomon."* Consequently, our identity in Him as His *Shulamite lover* leads us to a place of *peace* in Him, for *He is our peace;* He is the land of our inheritance, our rest, our *shalom;* and as we abide in Him, we become His rest, His inheritance, His peace, *His shalom.*

> *For He Himself is our peace, who has made both one, and has broken down the middle wall of separation, having abolished in His flesh the enmity, that is, the the law of commandments contained in ordinances, so as to create in Himself one new man from the two, thus making peace, and that He might reconcile them both to God in one body through the cross, thereby putting to death the enmity.*
>
> *Ephesians 2:14-16*

It is our abiding in this revelation of who He is and who we are in Him that girds us up for war as part of that awesome army which ravishes the very heart of our great Lord and King, Christ Jesus. *"For he who has entered into His rest has himself also ceased from his works as God did from His" (Hebrews 4:10)*. God will ultimately rest in His people as they come to rest in Him, for *we are His inheritance and He is ours.* As bride and groom, we are destined to *rest* in one another.

His *peace* is a place of rest from our own works and a place of empowerment where we learn to war *His war.* That is why He left us with this admonition, *"Peace I leave with you, My peace I give to you; not as the world gives do I give to you. Let not your heart be troubled, neither let it be afraid" (John 14:27)*. Our self-preserving wars will cease to the degree that we are able to abide in His peace, committing ourselves to *His wars*—the wars of the kingdom which advance the purposes of the kingdom.

The truth is that the Beloved has betrothed Himself to an *army* whose beauty is found in her total *dependence* upon Him as her Kinsman-Redeemer. To please this great lover of our souls, we must *abide* in this truth and obey Him out of a passionate devotion to who He is. *"We love Him because He first loved us" (I John 4:19),* and Jesus said, *"If you love Me, keep my commandments" (John 14:15)*. As we grow in our love for Him who first loved us, we come to believe what He says, and that transforms us into an *intimidating army of overcomers.*

Joel described this great and fearsome army of God as an army of *mighty men,* judging the powers of darkness with a *devouring fire*. This army *ravishes* the heart of God by its faith and devotion, in turn *ravaging* the ranks of the enemy by its *tenacious obedience* to God's commandments. As part of Christ's bride, we are called to be part of this magnificent army of the Lord described by Joel as,

> *...A people come, great and strong,*
> *The like of whom has never been;*
> *Nor will there ever be any such after them,*
> *Even for many successive generations.*
>
> *Joel 2:2b*

IX. A DANCE OF WAR

We are His dancing warriors
who dance the dance of the Shulamite.
It is a dance of worship and a dance of war.

Proclaim this among the nations:
"Prepare for war!
Wake up the mighty men,
Let all the men of war draw near,
Let them come up.
Beat your plowshares into swords
And your pruning hooks into spears;
Let the weak say, 'I am strong.' "
Joel 3:9-10

This spectacular dance of the Bride is a *dance of single-eyed devotion* as well as a glorious *dance of war* victoriously danced upon the heads of our enemies. This paradox of a worshiping bride who executes divine vengeance in the name of her God is a prophetic picture that is depicted repeatedly in Scripture.

Let the saints be joyful in glory;
Let them sing aloud on their beds.

Let the high praises of God be in their mouth,
And a two-edged sword in their hand,
To execute vengeance on the nations,
And punishments on the peoples;
To bind their kings with chains,
And their nobles with fetters of iron;
To execute on them the written judgment—
This honor have all His saints.

Praise the Lord!

Psalm 149:5-9

God is raising up an army who will execute judgment upon His *spiritual enemies* in His name. These *spiritual enemies* are the spiritual powers in high places which empower men and women to manifest the wickedness which fills the earth at this time. Yet God's judgments are sure, and as we abide in Him, we will enforce His judgments by not cooperating with the powers of darkness any longer, tearing down all of the high places in our lives which war against God and His kingdom. Thus, do we become part of that *army of mighty men,* ravaging the ranks of the enemy through an avid obedience to the Son and His every command.

> *The Lord gives voice before His army, For His camp is very great; For strong is the One who executes His word. For the day of the Lord is great and very terrible; Who can endure it?*
>
> *Joel 2:11*

Our *deliberate submission* to the Lord's will is the basis of our expression of this prophetic *dance of war* to which we are called. As His soldiers, we are subject to our Lord's every desire; thus does He train us to hear the subtleties of His voice that we might unwaveringly obey Him with eyes of faith and single-eyed devotion.

This is what we see evidenced in Abraham's life. His life in God prepared him to hear God's words to such a degree that he was able to "hear" God actually tell him to sacrifice his own son of promise. If Abraham had not been groomed by God to systematically die to self and embrace God's mysterious ways by *faith*, he would have never even *heard* such an outlandish request.

Similarly, to allow the Lord's voice to penetrate our dull of hearing carnality, we must crucify our ways that the life of God's ways might spring forth within us. Without this level of submission to God and His kingdom, there will be no ability to hear His voice which often makes *offensive* demands. We can never comply with such stipulations if we do not have eyes of faith. Faith in God and His ways which are beyond our ways is our *empowerment* to obey the Lord's hard words to us.

This type of obedience is birthed out of a *submissive* spirit, and it is the essence of the Bride's prophetic dance of war. *For within God's demands are hidden His divine strategies for the destruction of demonic strongholds within our lives and the lives of others.* Consequently, we see that God's purposes are mighty for the pulling down of strongholds, causing us to be conformed to His image for His purposes in us.

> *And we know that all things work together for good to those who love God, to those who are the called according to His purpose. For whom He foreknew, He also predestined to be conformed to the image of His Son, that He might be the firstborn among many brethren. Moreover whom He predestined, these He also called; whom He called, these He also justified; and whom He justified, these He also glorified. What then shall we say to these things? If God is for us, who can be against us?*
>
> Romans 8:28-31

God's purposes and ways are revealed to us as being *mighty for the pulling down of strongholds,* setting us free to fulfill the divine mandates laid before us. As we remain faithful to do all that the Lord has commanded of us, we will indeed dance a victorious dance of war upon the heads of our enemies. *That is our prophetic destiny as His people.*

Interestingly, as the children of Israel came up out of the wilderness ready to conquer the promised land, God's strategies for war were an enigma to their natural minds. Such *strategies* necessitate a *death* to some level of carnality and a *submission* to God's mysterious ways that victory might be acquired. Joshua and the children of Israel were instructed to walk around Jericho one time every day for six days and then seven times on the seventh day. God never told them *why*.

It is noteworthy that when the children of Israel were in disobedience in the wilderness, they also wandered around in circles, but for forty *long* years. Those particular *"circles"* were the expression of their *hard heartedness* toward God and His ways. Yet, these *"circles"* around Jericho were a *redemptive expression* of their *submitted* hearts, obeying the King of kings. Consequently, this redemptive act of obedience bore the fruit of *victory*, allowing them to ravage the stronghold of the enemy, dancing a victorious dance of war. That is what obedience to divine directives produces in our lives—*victory over our enemies.*

The Bride is called to dance a series of victorious conquests against her enemies. Those conquests are not a result of our own intricately laid out strategies. They are fruit born out of *obedience* to the Lord's divine orders. It takes *faith* to obey the Lord on this level, for His strategies can bear a stigma which our flesh violently wars against as His kingdom of light dramatically confronts the kingdom of darkness around us and in us.

To subjugate our self-life and its desires, we must have a divine perspective which fuels our faith concerning who God is and what His purposes are. We must have *eyes to see* and *ears to hear,* or we will miss our marching orders for the hour. Our God is truly a *consuming fire,* commanding His army and causing His kingdom to rule and reign on the earth as it does in heaven. As His bride, we are called to co-labor with Him in this divine aspiration. As such, *our obedience* becomes an expression of God's *consuming fire,* judging the powers of darkness which stand against our Lord's kingdom. Joel described such a fire issuing forth from God's great army.

A fire devours before them,
And behind them a flame burns;
The land is like the Garden of Eden before them,
And behind them a desolate wilderness;
Surely nothing shall escape them.
                              Joel 2:3

This is the army of the Lord, *a people great and strong, the like of whom has never been,* a consuming fire, dancing a *dance of war* upon God's enemies and judging the darkness by their *tenacious obedience* to the Son, loving not their lives to the death. ***This is the war dance of the Bride. This is the dance of the Shulamite.***

The Lord shall go forth like a mighty man;
He shall stir up His zeal like a man of war.
He shall cry out, yes, shout aloud;
He shall prevail against His enemies.
                              Isaiah 42:13

X. "WAITING" IS GOD'S STRATEGY

God's main strategy of war is waiting. Through it He establishes His sovereignty within our hearts, purifying the dance He has placed within us that we might enter into our full inheritance in Him.

Wait on the Lord,
And keep His way,
And He shall exalt you to inherit the land;
When the wicked are cut off, you shall see it.
Psalm 37:34

Once God enflames us with His purposes, giving us revelation of our need to war for them, He begins to purify us through the rigors of *waiting*. By causing us to wait on Him and His timing for war, *the futility of our ways is exposed,* permitting *His ways* to be established within us.

Waiting on God effectively causes us to be harnessed to His purposes and desires, bringing us to a place of *dependence upon Him.* It is this *dependence* which characterizes our role as soldiers in God's army. To rise to this prophetic call of the Bride, we must subject ourselves to His disciplines, humbling ourselves by submitting to God's timing and faithfully partaking of His spiritual provision. It is in our *dependence* that He is able to dictate His war strategies to us.

Waiting produces this type of dependence and brokenness as *our strategies* are systematically exposed and dismantled through the dealings of God and His blatant resistance to our ways. It is through such tactics that God establishes His sovereignty in our lives, causing us to literally lean upon Him for our every need. It is in such a place of vulnerability that we actually fulfill the prophetic picture of the Shulamite leaning upon her beloved as she is escorted out of the wilderness.

> *Who is this coming up from the wilderness,*
> *Leaning upon her beloved?*
> *I awakened you under the apple tree.*
> *There your mother brought you forth;*
> *There she who bore you brought you forth.*
>   *Song 8:5*

This is God's portrait of His end-time warriors. We are awakened to His passions under the *"apple tree"* in the *"garden of intimacy,"* and there God gives us His love, establishing us as His lovers and calling forth the *dance* which He put within us before the foundation of the world. As we are faithful to subject ourselves to His many chastenings, following Him into the wilderness and persevering in the times of waiting and pruning, we will indeed manifest as the desired Shulamite, leaning upon her beloved as an expression of intimacy and complete subjection.

God is committed to nurturing this type of allegiance and dependence in His bride that she might fulfill, not just her dance of love and devotion to Him, but her dance of war as well. To dance this victorious dance of war for the Groom, the Bride must be found sitting at His feet, hanging on His every word, devoted to His purposes. As His servants and soldiers in His army, He calls us to *wait on Him* that we might receive His prophetic strategies for victory. He is our great Warrior-King who leads us in and out of war victoriously.

> *"Therefore wait for Me," says the Lord,*
> *"Until the day I rise up for plunder;*
> *My determination is to gather the nations*
> *To My assembly of kingdoms,*
> *To pour on them My indignation,*
> *All My fierce anger;*
> *All the earth shall be devoured*
> *With the fire of My jealousy."*
> *Zephaniah 3:8*

His strategies are an enigma to those who are limited to the vision and purposes of their carnality. To embrace God's mysterious ways, we must be brought to the end of our ways. We must come to a place of complete and utter dependence upon the Son for our every provision. *He is the manna sent down from heaven.* As such, we must be found *leaning on Him,* attending to His every word that we might truly eat His provision. Without a revelation of our *neediness,* it is impossible to partake of Him, for we fail to see His provision for what it is; *it is life.*

Interestingly, *waiting* causes us to realize that we really aren't in control, though we may parade about as if we are. It also brings us to the revelation that we are not even called to be in control; *God is.* Waiting effectively exposes the frailties of our humanity, showing us the inconsistencies of our supposed *understandings* concerning God's kingdom. It exposes our hidden *unbelief* in God and who He is. The reality is that *God's ways are not our ways,* and waiting unveils that ever present reality, causing us to throw our hands in the air, crying out for Him to have His way. Thus, does God effectively establish His sovereignty in our hearts.

It is in the revelation of our innate weakness and desperate need for His provision that we are made strong. Our need drives us to Him, and He delights in giving strength to those who acknowledge their weakness.

He gives power to the weak,
And to those who have no might
He increases strength.

Even the youths shall faint and be weary,
And the young men shall utterly fall,
But those who wait on the Lord
Shall renew their strength;
They shall mount up with wings like eagles,
They shall run and not be weary,
They shall walk and not faint.

Isaiah 40:29-31

God not only delights in giving grace to the humble who seek Him, but He delights in actually *conquering* His foes with the foolish and weak who have come to a revelation of God's sure salvation for them. *"But God has chosen the foolish things of the world to put to shame the wise, and God has chosen the weak things of the world to put to shame the things which are mighty;" (I Corinthians 1:27).*

Our strength to accomplish those tasks which He has laid before us quite literally flows from the Master as we learn to *wait* on His provision and *feed* upon Him. *Waiting* leads us to a place of *needing* to feed upon the Son, and *feeding* upon the Son leads us to a place of *abiding* in the Son. Christ said of Himself,

For My flesh is food indeed, and My blood is drink indeed. For he who eats My flesh and drinks My blood abides in Me, and I in Him.

John 6:55-56

Though God causes us to wait on Him, regardless of what *we* think or want, that does not ensure that we will actually enter into the type of *"waiting"* that He is desiring of us. God's desired *waiting* involves *faith* and heightened *expectancy*, for it possesses the knowledge that God's intervention is our *only* hope.

Thus, do we look avidly for His provision every day, listening intently for His voice.

> *I wait for the Lord, my soul waits,*
> *And in His word I do hope.*
> *My soul waits for the Lord*
> *More than those who watch for the morning—*
> *Yes; more than those who watch for the morning.*
> *Psalm 130:5-6*

This type of *waiting* which God desires is not characterized by *a passive resignation*; for passivity is a sign of *unbelief* and *loss of vision*. Our waiting is to be characterized by faith in God and what He has said. However, all too often, God's seasons of waiting can cause people to lose their vision or to even become *offended* at God for not doing what He said He would do according to their understanding of the times and seasons. That type of offense with God can cause many to drop by the wayside in a huff with their arms crossed in disgust. Unfortunately, that is where much of the Body of Christ lives its entire life in God—*offended with His ways* and not able to confront such an issue with repentance.

Some express this offense with God through chronic apathy in spiritual things, pacifying themselves with religious rituals; others express their offense by blasting ahead in the power of their own souls, actually setting up their own *ministries*, successfully numbing themselves to any need to actually hear from God any further. Out of offense they have turned away from the divine injunction to daily *feed* upon God's very words as manna sent from heaven. Instead, they live upon the *old manna*, deeply offended by those who *apparently* hear God's voice and are feeding upon His provision on a regular basis, living the vibrant prophetic lifestyle of an *overcomer*. Such a prophetic lifestyle is an affront to those who have drawn back in unbelief *"having a form of godliness but denying its power"* (II Timothy 3:5).

To effectively grow in God and live the life of an *overcomer*, our offenses with Him must be dealt with honestly so that our misconceptions about God and ourselves can be corrected by the *truth*. That is why *waiting* is such an effective strategy used by God to establish His sovereignty in our hearts; otherwise we would keep living under the deception that He already was sovereign in our lives. Yet God knows better, and He needs to expose our self deceptions to us, so that we can mature in the ways of the kingdom and become those mighty soldiers in His army of truth, leaning upon the breast of the Beloved who reigns supreme.

It should be noted that not just the saints are

required *to wait on God*. All of creation *waits* on Him as well. Even the wicked *wait* on Him for His judgments to be made manifest. The Lord says of Himself,

> *My righteousness is near,*
> *My salvation has gone forth,*
> *And my arms will judge the peoples;*
> *The coastlands will wait upon me,*
> *And on My arm they will trust.*
> *Isaiah 51:5*

The strategies of the kingdom are hidden in the discipline of *waiting on God,* for it is in *the waiting* that we discover His ways. It is in *the waiting* that we discover *Him.* He is our commander, and when we discover Him in His sovereign role as ruler over *all* of creation, we will *hear* His voice giving orders to His great army; for He is indeed the great Warrior-King of heaven and earth. *"The Lord is a man of war: the Lord is His name" (Exodus 15:3).* Because of His greatness, what can we do but wait for Him? He is our only refuge.

> *Are there any among the idols of the nations*
>   *that can cause rain?*
> *Or can the heavens give showers?*
> *Are You not He, O Lord our God?*
> *Therefore we will wait for You,*
> *Since You have made all these.*
> *Jeremiah 14:22*

As part of God's army, we are called to diligently attend to the *thunder of His voice*, listening for His direction and then joining our voices to His voice in full agreement with His purposes and desires. As our voices declare His sovereign pleasure, all of creation will quake and tremble before us, for His creative voice will resonate from within us as we speak. May we all aspire to rise to its call through faith in Him who woos us to His side for the battle of the ages.

He will swallow up death forever,
And the Lord God will wipe away
* tears from all faces;*
The rebuke of His people
He will take away from the earth;
For the Lord has spoken.

And it will be said in that day:
"Behold, this is our God;
We have waited for Him, and He will save us.
This is the Lord;
We have waited for Him;
We will be glad and rejoice in His salvation."
                                    Isaiah 25:8-9

XI. THE CALL OF THE KINGDOM

Waiting causes us to hear the call of the kingdom...
a call to life...
His life...
our death...
His servanthood...
a call to follow the Lamb with abandon...

...These are the ones who follow the Lamb wherever He goes. These were redeemed from among men, being firstfruits to God and to the Lamb. And in their mouth was found no deceit, for they are without fault before the throne of God.

Revelation 14:4-5

There is a *call* in the kingdom which needs to undergird all that we do for Him, causing us to partake of His character. As servants who are called to walk as He walked, we must possess His nature which was that of a *servant*, a servant who walked in the fruit of the Spirit: *love, joy, peace, longsuffering, kindness, goodness, faithfulness, gentleness, and self-control (Galatians 5:22-23).* When evidenced *genuinely* from a true servant of God, these are qualities which literally *disarm* the powers of darkness. The genuineness of Jesus' life here on earth enabled Him to do just that. He disarmed powers and principalities by the simple manifestation of such traits, which was an obedient expression of His servanthood unto the will of the Father.

Such kingdom traits actually have the power to thwart the purposes of the enemy. That is why Paul admonishes us to not repay evil for evil *(Romans 12:17),* but to live peaceably with all men, resting in God's sovereign rulership and remembering that vengeance is indeed the Lord's *(Romans 12:19).*

Therefore
  "If your enemy is hungry, feed him;
  If he is thirsty, give him a drink;
  For in so doing you will heap coals
    of fire on his head."
Do not be overcome by evil, but overcome evil
    with good.
                                   Romans 12:20-21

These are some of the paradoxes of the kingdom. We must live by such truths, or we will find ourselves warring according to the ways of the world, unintentionally setting ourselves at odds with the purposes of the kingdom and with *God Himself.*

To truly manifest such glorious and powerful fruit of the kingdom of light we will need to die to *our ways... our vengeance... our desires.* We have been called to lay down our lives and humbly take on the mysterious ways of our Lord and His kingdom. These ways are not futile and passive, but mighty for the pulling down of strongholds and the perpetuation of God's kingdom in the earth.

Christ Himself instructed us in the paradoxical warfare of the kingdom, detailing explicit examples concerning this kingdom principle of refusing to return evil for evil.

But I tell you not to resist an evil person.
But whoever slaps you on your right cheek,
turn the other to him also.
If anyone wants to sue you and take away
your tunic, let him have your cloak also.
And whoever compels you to go one mile,
go with him two.
Give to him who asks you, and from him who
wants to borrow from you do not turn away.
You have heard that it was said,
"You shall love your neighbor and hate your enemy."
But I say to you, love your enemies, bless those who
curse you, do good to those who hate you,   ·
and pray for those who spitefully use you and

persecute you, that you may be sons of your Father in
heaven; for He makes His sun rise on the evil and on
the good, and sends rain on the just and on the unjust.

Matthew 5:39-45

Christ's instructions paint a picture of a kingdom that operates in absolute contradiction to any earthly kingdom we may have witnessed. God's kingdom is based on the reality that the one and only true God of heaven and earth *reigns supreme*, and because of that, we as His heirs do not have to *react* to evil. Instead, we *respond* in righteousness because of the perspective of the kingdom of which we are a part, just as Jesus did. It is in this fashion that we *disarm* the power of the enemy in any given situation, stopping the perpetuation of evil.

This is the life of the kingdom, a life of *love, joy, peace, longsuffering, kindness, goodness, faithfulness, gentleness, and self-control.* This life was made possible by God's righteous sacrifice, releasing the blood of the Lamb to speak on behalf of the purposes of His kingdom. Consequently, we don't have to *defend* God or His kingdom; His kingdom *reigns regardless.* We are called to merely follow Him. As His servants, He will lead us into *His battles*; for it is *He* who girds us up for battle—those battles which fulfill *His purposes.*

Does this mean that we passively watch as evil

goes unchecked? Absolutely not! As we walk in the Spirit, hearing the *sounds of the kingdom,* we will surely hear the sound of God's *spiritual shofar,* calling us to battle, and the success of our warfare will depend on our ability to believe what God has said and done for us; for our victory is found in His provision for us and our ability to access it by *faith.*

When we live life out of the truths of the kingdom, we are no longer subject to the empty taunts of the enemy. The enemy's lies are only empowered by our belief in them, for our agreement with the enemy subjugates us to his evil ways; however, if we have chosen to submit to the ways of the Righteous Judge, Christ Jesus, *eating* His words to us and *drinking* His life blood for full redemption and empowerment to live the life of an overcomer, then our stand of faith in God's words to us will hold back the perpetuation of evil in our lives and in the lives of others with whom we interact.

Because of the redemptive nature of the kingdom, *curses* that are released against us will be turned to *blessings* as we walk in His redemptive light, for He redeems and judges all things that we give to Him. Even the trials that come our way possess redemptive value as we are given another opportunity to *overcome* our enemy and thereby increase the anointing of God upon our lives; for God dwells with those who abide in Him and obey His mandates. They are the *overcomers* who actually perpetuate His kingdom through their simple acts of obedience.

This is the dance of the kingdom, a dance of *servanthood and humility*, disarming the powers of darkness by manifesting the very truths of the kingdom which have been imparted to us by Christ's own life blood. It is His life blood which leads us into the truths of the kingdom, and in the process, strongholds of the enemy are undermined, causing them to collapse.

That is our dance as His bride, a *kingdom dance of love, joy, peace, longsuffering, kindness, goodness, faithfulness, gentleness, and self-control* in the midst of a wicked and perverse world which hates us because it hated Him. Since the blood ever speaks on our behalf and God's judgments reign supreme, we can rest in His ways, following Him wherever He leads, speaking the *language of Judah*—the language of the kingdom—and standing before His throne in total purity.

To gain this identity as an overcoming servant who stands before the throne of the living God in purity and acceptance will cost us something—*our death*. We will have to lay down our lives and our former identities, *ceasing the dances that we have danced in the past*. Some of these dances have insidiously camouflaged themselves within the expression of our Christian lives, bringing defilement and allowing the enemy to taunt us with bondages from which we *still* have not been delivered. The answer is *death* to our ways. *Out of our death comes Christ's redemptive life,* a life of humility and servanthood.

> *Let this mind be in you which was also in Christ Jesus, who, being in the form of God, did not consider it robbery to be equal with God, but made Himself of no reputation, taking the form of a bondservant, and coming in the likeness of men. And being found in appearance as a man, He humbled Himself and became obedient to the point of death, even the death of the cross.*
>
> *Philippians 2:5-8*

We are called to humble ourselves, taking on His nature. That can only happen as we stand in the power of the blood, allowing it to silence the voices which speak against God's purposes and which woo us to pursue our own way. Even though His ways are not naturally our ways, we can *choose* to make them our ways, crucifying our desires and embracing His. This is what being *"conformed to his death" (Philippians 3:10)* involves ... death... *our death.*

> *I have been crucified with Christ; it is no longer I who live, but Christ lives in me; and the life which I now live in the flesh I live by the Son of God, who loved me and gave Himself for me.*
>
> *Galatians 2:20*

Before the *dance of the Shulamite* can come to fullness with a pure expression, we must dance our personal *dance of death*, turning away from the other seductive *dances* within our lives. Those dances can involve *spiritual ambition, lust for power and prominence, love for money, love of mundane things, etc.* These dances are counterfeit dances birthed out of the kingdom of darkness that often find expression in our spiritual lives, but such "dances" have no place in God's kingdom. Therefore, God will chasten us and resist us until such defilement has been exposed and brought into subjection to the testimony of the blood of Christ.

Our personal dance of death, choreographed by the King of kings, awaits our participation on the stage of life. That dance will most definitely be tortuous and painful to our fleshly ways, but it must be performed, that the dance of life, the *dance of the Shulamite*, might break forth, swallowing death up in victory and bringing glory and honor to the choreographer, Christ Jesus, the Beloved.

As the law of sin and death is overcome through our own subjection to the cross of Christ, the kingdom of God is extended, and that is the essence of the kingdom—to become His servants, extending His kingdom throughout the earth and overcoming the very sting of death with the abundant life of the kingdom here and now. May we each dance our own *dance of death* to our carnal ways that the life of the *dance of the Shulamite* might bud forth in grand victory and splendor.

"O Death, where is your sting?
O Hades, where is your victory?"

The sting of death is sin,
And the strength of sin is the law.

But thanks be to God, who gives us
the victory through our Lord Jesus Christ.

I Corinthians 15:55-57

XII. THE PREVAILING SOUND
OF THE KINGDOM

Waiting awakens us to the subtle sounds of the kingdom...the sound of the Beloved speaking His desires to His bride, imparting His heart to her.

> *I sleep, but my heart is awake;*
> *It is the voice of my beloved!*
> *He knocks, saying,*
> *"Open for me, my sister, my love,*
> *My dove, my perfect one;*
> *For my head is covered with dew,*
> *My locks with the drops of the night."*
>
> Song 5:2

There are many sounds in the kingdom, and it is in the times of *waiting* that our ears begin to hear them. Some of these sounds include: *the vibrant, redemptive sound of the blood speaking on our behalf*, awakening us to a deeper revelation and application of its testimony in our lives; *the call of the kingdom to servanthood;* and *the reassuring sound of the*

Beloved's voice, gently reminding us of His great love for His people. It is this sound, the sound of His affirmations of love to us, that I regard as the **prevailing sound of the kingdom**, undergirding all other sounds. This is the sound that carries us through the hardest of times, transforming us into His lovesick bride, consumed with His desires. Without an acquaintance with this special sound, our identities in Him remain shallow, keeping us far from the Beloved's intimate embrace; yet, knowing His voice is most assuredly a defining characteristic of *His sheep*.

During the many seasons of our lives, but especially the times of waiting, God teaches us to discern the many different ways that He speaks to us. If we only live by His written word and His perceived "spoken" word to us, we will miss the deeper truths that are only imparted to us as we gain *His heart*.

The mysterious ways of our God can only be discerned as we gain a revelation of His heart. This specific revelation comes as we are driven through trials and testings to lay our heads upon His chest in an attitude of brokenness and submission. Such *spiritual posturing* allows us to hear His heartbeat and become acquainted with His ways; for it is in our heartfelt response to His passions that we come to discern His desires for us, and it is out of an understanding of His desires that we "hear" His directives to us—either specifically or implied.

It is then that we begin to walk out our relationship with Him based on a passionate devotion to His purposes. Consequently, there is an executing of His *spoken and unspoken desires*, for we have moved beyond the mentality of a mere servant who merely does what he is told, to a *friend and lover of God* who is consumed with the Beloved's desires and ways, looking for a way to please Him out of a pure love for Him and His ways.

It is this mindset that sets us free to hear the heartbeat of the kingdom which revolves around *reconciliation and friendship with God.* As we begin to understand that underlying truth in the kingdom, we come into new levels of service to our King. We begin to comprehend a lifestyle that He is requiring of us. It is a lifestyle that causes us to look and act like Him, listening and responding to the many *sounds of His kingdom.*

It is when we begin to embrace this truth that our ears are opened to hear His requests of us to which we have been deaf in the past. These requests are strategic in bringing about a deeper death to our self-life that His resurrection power might come forth, for the abundant life springs forth from our willing death to self. That is a death we cannot orchestrate, because we don't know ourselves sufficiently, but He knows us through and through.

This *death* to carnality comes as a consequence of

falling more deeply in love with Him. Our eyes begin to see the glory and wonder of the kingdom as we live and eat of His words to us. That level of passion for the Son causes us to turn away from the things of this life and the carnality of the natural realm, choosing rather to live life out of the *spiritual truths* from which we have been feeding. Paul had a revelation of this mysterious type of *death and life* to which we are called to walk within the dynamics of the kingdom.

> *Yet indeed I also count all things loss for the excellence of the knowledge of Christ Jesus my Lord, for whom I have suffered the loss of all things, and count them as rubbish, that I may gain Christ and be found in Him, not having my own righteousness, which is from the law, but that which is through faith in Christ, the righteousness which is from God by faith; that I may know Him and the power of His resurrection, and the fellowship of His sufferings, being conformed to His death, if, by any means, I may attain to the resurrection from the dead.*
> *Philippians 3:8-11*

Death to self on this level will cause a servitude of complete abandoned love for the Son of God to express itself in our lives. This is a servitude that is content not only in doing things *for* the Beloved, but in *waiting at His feet*, enjoying His presence for who He is. This new level of servitude flows from an increased revelation of our identity in Him, found by *abiding* in His presence and becoming one with Him in purpose and deed.

This transformation from a mere servant to a *friend and lover of God* happens in the times of *waiting*. The waiting causes us to hear His heart as we sit at His feet, listening for His voice. It is there that His many mysteries are unfolded to us as His friends. *"No longer do I call you servants, for a servant does not know what his master is doing; but I have called you friends, for all things that I heard from My Father I have made known to you" (John 15:15).*

The essence of our servitude to Christ is that of *friendship*. We are called to be friends and lovers of God, who live not just by His written and spoken word to us, but by the *spirit and heart* behind those words. This reality will cause us to live life out of the truth of who God is and who we are in Him, as opposed to living life out of a mere knowledge of God. This is what causes us to be identified as His people.

> *But this is the covenant that I will make with the house of Israel after those days, says the Lord: I will put My law in their minds, and write it on their hearts; and I will be their God, and they shall be My people.*
>
> *Jeremiah 31:33*

Through our friendship with God, we are allowed to *see* into His secrets that we might begin to *hear* His hidden desires, which reveal His mandates to us as His people called by His name. Many of those mandates are unspoken, but vibrate as *sounds in the kingdom* that we hear and obey out of the revelation of His mysteries. It is in this manner that we live by the voice of the Spirit, allowing God to write His law upon our hearts that we might dance the dance of a consecrated life, dancing to the very notes and sounds that flow from His desires.

The Beloved's all consuming desire is for His bride's companionship and her ultimate perfection. That prophetic desire prevails as the mighty sound of all sounds in the kingdom of our God. It is truly the prophetic melody of this great desire which gives cadence and momentum to the coveted dance of devotion that we are called to dance unto Him as His lovers and friends.

The Lord has appeared of old to me, saying:
"Yes, I have loved you with an everlasting love;
Therefore with lovingkindness I have drawn you.
Again I will build you, and you shall be rebuilt,
O virgin of Israel!
You shall again be adorned with your tambourines,
And shall go forth in the dances of those who rejoice.
You shall yet plant vines on the mountains of
    Samaria;
The planters shall plant and eat them as ordinary
    food.
For there shall be a day
When the watchmen will cry on Mount Ephraim,

'Arise, and let us go up to Zion,
To the Lord our God.' "

Jeremiah 31:3-6

XIII. HIS PROPHETIC INVITATION
TO THE BRIDE

His prophetic invitation to His bride is one of joining our voices with His voice, crying out for His beloved Israel to come forth...a joining of the natural and the spiritual...a completion of a prophetic picture of Jew and Gentile becoming one in Him as His bride.

For the Lord will have mercy on Jacob, and will still choose Israel, and settle them in their own land. The strangers will be joined with them, and they will cling to the house of Jacob.

Isaiah 14:1

As our dance unto Him progresses beyond the obedience of a *servant* to the passion of a *friend and lover of God,* knowing His heart and living life out of *His heartbeat,* we will surely hear Him calling us to go to the people groups of the earth to extend His rule; for it is when we truly know *His heart* that we can be trusted with *His mandates.* Thus, it is crucial that we

97

allow Him to impart His heart to us and write His ways on our hearts that we might actually suggest to Him what He has already put on our hearts—the conquest of imparting His kingdom to others. *That is the intercession of the Bride, speaking the Beloved's heart back to Him.*

As we grow in intimacy with the Lord, His heart for the nations will be increasingly imparted to us, and His Spirit will surely reveal the times and the seasons of His kingdom that we might labor with Him in His conquests.

The voice of my beloved!
Behold, he comes
Leaping upon the mountains,
Skipping upon the hills.
My beloved is like a gazelle or a young stag.
Behold, he stands behind our wall;
He is looking through the windows,
Gazing through the lattice.

My beloved spoke, and said to me:
"Rise up, my love, my fair one,
And come away.
For lo, the winter is past,
The rain is over and gone.
The flowers appear on the earth;
The time of singing has come,

And the voice of the turtledove
Is heard in our land.
The fig tree puts forth her green figs,
And the vines with the tender grapes
Give a good smell.
Rise up, my love, my fair one,
And come away!
"O my dove, in the clefts of the rock,
In the secret places of the cliff,
Let me see your face,
Let me hear your voice;
For your voice is sweet,
And your face is lovely."

Song 2:8-14

This is the Beloved's *prophetic invitation* to us that we might partake of His heart for His people and join our voices with His in intercession. He desires that we would be as zealous for the *consecration and empowerment* of the Bride as He is. This Bride will be comprised of *all* nations, but is specifically represented in the earth by natural Israel--a picture of a "peculiar people" gathered from all nations who are being transformed into the people of God. Scripturally, the "fig tree" is a prophetic picture of the Bride as she comes into her fullness, identifying herself with natural Israel, a physical picture of a greater spiritual reality being played out in the corporate people of God across the globe.

As we gain increased revelation of natural Israel's purpose, we will begin to join our voices to the cry of the Beloved who cries for the veil to be removed from His Jewish people that they might see Him as their Redeemer and King. Interestingly, as natural Israel comes to a revelation of the true Messiah, Yeshua ha Meshiach (Christ's Hebraic name), and His sacrificial death, so will the Church grow in her own revelation of the Son of God. Indeed, the Church needs further revelation of the Son that she might be transformed into that glorious bride for whom He is returning. Consequently, we see that the *heartbeat of the kingdom* is the wooing of the Bride by the Beloved that she might enter into her destiny as a co-laborer in His kingdom, tending His *garden*, crying out in intercession for what *He desires*.

As the truth of this penetrates the Church, we will have our eyes focused intently on the "budding of the fig tree." This "budding" can be measured by the events transpiring in natural Israel; for the Church has indeed been grafted into this spiritual "olive tree" of which Israel is the *firstfruit of the root*. As such, our call is to intercede and war for natural Israel to come back from the *dead* that she might rejuvenate the whole tree.

For if you were cut out of the olive tree which is wild by nature, and were grafted contrary to nature into a cultivated olive tree, how much more will these, who are natural branches, be grafted into their own olive tree? For I do not desire, brethren, that you should be ignorant of this mystery, lest you should be wise in your own opinion, that blindness in part has happened to Israel until the fullness of the Gentiles has come in.

Romans 11:24-25

Astoundingly, natural Israel has been blinded to who the Messiah is, so that *all* nations might enter into this great salvation. Consider the reality of natural Israel's "death" and its dramatic release of *life* to the nations; as such, what will her *life from the dead* release to the world and especially to the Church which has been grafted into her inheritance *(Romans 11:15)*? The Church itself has been blind to the relevance of a *Jewish* Messiah and the birthright purchased for us, causing our identity as His bride to be obscured by lies and distortions, due in part to our basic misunderstanding of the role of the Jew and natural Israel in relation to the Church. In fact, the Church in ignorance and blindness to the truth has been a misguided persecutor of the Jew.

As natural Israel has resisted entering into God's covenant of faith in the provision of the Son, so the Church has resisted the walk of faith, and Paul clearly writes that it is only by *faith* that we enter into covenant with God. Therefore, the true *Israel* of God are those who partake of the new covenant of grace by *faith* in the provisional death of the Son of God. There is no other way to be saved from God's wrath. That is why Paul could say, *"For they are not all Israel who are of Israel,"* (Romans 9:6b).

> *For you are all sons of God through faith in Christ Jesus. For as many of you as were baptized into Christ have put on Christ. There is neither Jew nor Greek, there is neither slave nor free, there is neither male nor female; for you are all one in Christ Jesus. And if you are Christ's, then you are Abraham's seed, and heirs according to the promise.*
> *Galatians 3:26-29*

As the "grafted-in ones" our injunction is to cry out for the "branches," represented by natural Israel, to awaken to the saving grace found in Messiah Yeshua, and to *"...remember that you do not support the root, but the root supports you" (Romans 11:18b).* As such, natural Israel is the Church's elder brother; our tutor in the faith, if we will let her teach us. *Therefore, our increased understanding of the Church's identification with natural Israel will actually facilitate the unveiling of the mystery of the Bride of Yeshua in the last days; for the Bride is indeed that completed picture of a redeemed Israel, made up of Jew and Gentile.*

The Beloved's heart beats hard after the unveiling of His bride, and that bride is incomplete without the reviving of the "branches" of natural Israel. He desires to impart this truth to us who serve Him. This is why He woos us to come away with Him that we might gain His heart for those things He desires. The truth is that

His eyes are ever on His "garden," watching His "vines." In fact, if we want to find our Beloved, we will be sure to find Him focused on *His garden*, brooding over His people, and natural Israel is part of that picture. The Shulamite declares this reality to the daughters of Jerusalem who are seeking Him as well,

My beloved has gone to his garden,
To the beds of spices,
To feed his flock in the gardens,
And to gather lilies.
                    Song 6:2-3

It is interesting that it is among the "lilies," those who have entered into intimacy with the Beloved, that He chooses to feed His flock; and it is the Shulamite, the Beloved's bride, who knows this mystery. In fact, she reiterates her identity as *His lover*, reminding us that *intimacy* does indeed preclude the unveiling of mysteries in the kingdom.

I am my beloved's.
And my beloved is mine.
He feeds his flock among the lilies.
                    Song 6:3

The Shulamite so identifies with the Beloved and His desires that she, too, visits His garden, not only to find Him, but *"to see whether the vine had budded and the pomegranates had bloomed"(Song 6:11b).*

Prophetically, as the vine "buds" and the Church comes into her true identity as His lover and bride, so will her priestly attributes manifest, represented by the *blooming of the pomegranates*. The Bride's priesthood will indeed parallel that of her groom's when He walked the earth, ministering in miraculous signs and wonders to the needy and the brokenhearted.

This prophetic invitation to co-labor with our groom is going forth now to those who have ears to hear. Yet, only those who have been wooed into the chambers of intimacy and have partaken of the Beloved's heart for a united Israel to come to fullness will be prepared for such dramatic displays of power and anointing.

It is our time in His chambers, nestled away in a wilderness of His choosing, that these truths are instilled in us. To the degree that we are faithful in these times of testing and chastening will He be able to use us for such kingdom purposes; for He does indeed long to hear the voice of the Bride's intercession, for *her voice is sweet (Song 8:14)*.

This *bridal intercession* will be built upon a revelation of His heart's cry for reconciliation with His creation and the preparation of a bride worthy of Him. Hearing this cry of the Beloved's heart will position us to participate in His endeavors through intercession, repeating back to the Beloved His desire for the Jewish people, as well as all nations, to enter into fullness as

His consecrated people, *Israel*. Such petitions are the catalyst in releasing His favor upon us, causing Him to actually arise in our behalf.

> *You will arise and have mercy on Zion;*
> *For the time to favor her,*
> *Yes, the set time, has come.*
> *For Your servants take pleasure in her stones,*
> *And show favor to her dust.*
> *So the nations shall fear the name of the Lord,*
> *And all the kings of the earth Your glory.*
> *For the Lord shall build up Zion;*
> *He shall appear in His glory.*
> *He shall regard the prayer of the destitute,*
> *And shall not despise their prayer.*
> *Psalm 102:13-17*

As His people, we are invited to become one with Him as His bride, proclaiming His will. We are called to watch over His beloved Israel with prophetic eagle eyes, taking our place on the wall of His spiritual city.

> *I have set watchmen on your walls, O Jerusalem;*
> *They shall never hold their peace day or night.*
> *You who make mention of the Lord, do not keep silent,*
> *And give Him no rest till He establishes*
> *And till He makes Jerusalem a praise in the earth.*
> *Isaiah 62:6-7*

Therefore, does the intercession of the Bride

become her prophetic proclamation of purpose and desire for the Beloved and His kingdom, crying out for Him to actually fulfill His desire toward Jerusalem, a prophetic picture of the Bride. It is in that intercession that the Bride will enter into the fullness of her identity as the intimate lover of the Beloved, Yeshua ha Meshiach, desiring only what He desires. Thus will she run to *His garden*, crying out for Him to come and fulfill His desires in the earth, for it is in the fullness of the desires of the Beloved that the Bride will find her fullness as well. The birthing of that desire in the Bride will produce a fragrance that will incite the Beloved to fulfill His purposes in the earth and return for His cherished bride. *That fragrance is the prophetic intercession of the Bride.* May we conceive this desire in our spiritual wombs, causing us to abide in His garden, satisfying His every longing. ***This truly is a captivating aroma of the Bride's dance of devotion—intercession for the Beloved's desires, petitioning Him to do all that He longs to do in the earth...***

I am my beloved's,
And his desire is toward me,
Come, my beloved,
Let us go forth to the field;
Let us lodge in the villages.
Let us get up early to the vineyards;
Let us see if the vine has budded,
Whether the grape blossoms are open,

And the pomegranates are in bloom.
There I will give you my love.
The mandrakes give off a fragrance,
And at our gates are pleasant fruits,
All manner, new and old,
Which I have laid up for you, my beloved.

Song 7:10-13

Empowered

For Conquest...

At His Side,

As His Bride

XIV. THE ANOINTING OF THE BRIDE

There are three that bear witness to the truths of the kingdom here on earth. Those three are weapons which empower us to extend the kingdom of God throughout the earth as His worshiping warriors.

For there are three that bear witness in heaven: the Father, the Word, and the Holy Spirit; and these three are one.

And there are three that bear witness on earth: the Spirit, the water, and the blood; these three agree as one.

1 John 5:7-8

Since our *kingdom mandate* is to minister unto our God, extending His kingdom throughout the earth, God has made elaborate and wondrous provision for this mighty task. That provision is found in none other than Himself, and is extended to us through *His anointing*. It is His anointing that brings us into His presence, and it is His anointing that empowers us to fulfill His desires. As God's anointing rests upon our lives, the truths of His kingdom are manifest. Within His anointing of us do we find the expression of the Godhead—the Father, Son, and Holy Spirit. In the natural, the manifestation of such truths is prophetically represented in the *water,* the *blood,* and the *oil* anointings.

These three "witnesses" gird us up for our three roles in the kingdom as new covenant *prophets, priests,* and *kings;* and as such, they represent aspects of God's provision and empowerment for us in our actualization of these roles. Since these three "witnesses" actually empower us to fulfill these kingdom callings, I will reference them as "anointings." Quite simply, when God *anoints* us for something, He *empowers* us to accomplish what He has asked of us. With this in mind, increased revelation of these three "anointings" will indeed enable us to more powerfully walk in the fullness of our roles as God's *prophets, priests,* and *kings,* causing us to bear more of His presence to a dying world. That is the essence of *the anointing*–more of *Him;* and that is the essence of our dance unto Him. It is a dance that releases His presence and anointing into the earth.

The Blood Anointing

The *blood anointing* is necessary for us to find acceptance in His sight. Without the atoning blood of the Son *anointing us,* or empowering us with *His righteousness,* we are lost and have no hope; but with it, we are the sons and daughters of the King of kings.

Being justified freely by His grace through the redemption that is in Christ Jesus, whom God set forth as a propitiation by His blood, through faith, to demonstrate His righteousness, because in His forbearance God had passed over the sins that were previously committed, to demonstrate at the present time His righteousness, that He might be just and the justifier of the one who has faith in Jesus.

Romans 3:24-26

It is indeed His blood which empowers us to carry His name as our own, representing Him to the nations. It literally enables us to come before Him, to minister to others about Him, and to conquer powers and principalities at His leading. It is His blood that leads us into our callings as *prophets, priests,* and *kings*; and it is His blood that empowers us to prophetically minister unto Him, one another, and the nations, extending His kingdom through our obedience, and likewise, *ruling and reigning* with Him here on earth.

Coming to Him as a living stone, rejected indeed by men, but chosen by God and precious, you also, as living stones, are being built up a spiritual house, a holy priesthood, to offer up spiritual sacrifices acceptable to God through Jesus Christ.

I Peter 2:4-5

The blood is the anointing which *births* us into the kingdom, for without it the other anointings have no place or power in our lives. It is the blood of Christ which establishes us in the kingdom as sons and daughters destined to an inheritance in Him.

Blessed be the God and Father of our Lord Jesus Christ, who according to His abundant mercy has begotten us again to a living hope through the resurrection of Jesus Christ from the dead, to an inheritance incorruptible and undefiled and that does not fade away, reserved in heaven for you, who are kept by the power of God through faith for salvation ready to be revealed in the last time.

I Peter 1:3-5

As His sons and daughters, washed in His blood, we are given the right to access His throne because of His provisional atonement for us.

Therefore, brethren, having boldness to enter the Holiest by the blood of Jesus, by a new and living way which He consecrated for us, through the veil, that is, His flesh, and having a High Priest over the house of God, let us draw near with a true heart in full assurance of faith, having our hearts sprinkled from an evil conscience and our bodies washed with pure water.

Hebrews 10:19-22

The Beloved washes us with His blood as well as with the *water of His words* to us. The water and the blood work together in preparing us to enter into His presence that we might fulfill our purposes in Him. Though the blood of Christ is our *only* covering for sin, the washing of the water of the word causes us to see where we fall short that we might appropriate the blood. That blood is appropriated as we choose to submit to *His covering* for us and turn away from *our covering.* That process involves a *death to self* as we choose God's ways over our own, following the Son in the life of obedience He modeled for us while He was here on earth. **Though the blood purchases our birthright into the kingdom; it is *our obedience to the Lord*, joined in agreement with His blood that empowers us for our purposes in Him, causing us to be victorious over our enemies.** Such a sacrifice is our reasonable service to our Lord.

> *I beseech you therefore, brethren, by the mercies of God, that you present your bodies a living sacrifice, holy, acceptable to God, which is your reasonable service. And do not be conformed to this world, but be transformed by the renewing of your mind, that you may prove what is that good and acceptable and perfect will of God.*
>
> *Romans 12:1-2*

We are called to die daily to our own desires, just as our Lord did. This death releases a *spiritual sacrifice* that mingles with the blood of the Son, sending up *"a sweet-smelling aroma, an acceptable sacrifice, well pleasing to God" (Philippians 4:18b).* Paul said that we are to carry about in our bodies *"...the dying of the Lord Jesus, that the life of Jesus also may be manifested in our body. For we who live are always delivered to death for Jesus' sake, that the life of Jesus also may be manifested in our mortal flesh. So then death is working in us, but life in you" (II Corinthians 4:10-12).*

This is the *death* that releases the *dance of the Shulamite* to come forth, for it is a dance of *death* to self but a dance of *life* to God and His kingdom. Without the *blood anointing* of His *atoning death* on the cross combined with our own *death to self*, the *dance of the Shulamite* will be greatly hindered.

The Water Anointing

The *water anointing* is commonly associated with the ritual washing known as *water baptism* which we are instructed to do as an outward testimony of our choice to die to ourselves and live to God. *"Therefore we were buried with Him through baptism into death, that just as Christ was raised from the dead by the glory of the Father, even so we also should walk in newness of life" (Romans 6:4).* This baptism grew out of the Jewish ritual of washing or *baptism* which was observed in connection with *repentance* and a desire to

116

come before God with a clean heart. The old covenant priests were instructed to observe many ritual washings in order to come into God's presence. In fact, their failure to attend to such a requirement could cost them their lives. Concerning the priests, the Lord told Moses,

When they go into the tabernacle of meeting, or when they come near the altar to minister, to burn an offering made by fire to the Lord, they shall wash with water, lest they die.

Exodus 30:20

Ritual cleansings were representations of a need for *inner purity*. The blood sacrifices for worship and atonement were unacceptable without the repeated cleansing by water which prepared the priest to make these offerings.

Christ anointed His disciples with this priestly washing at the Passover before His blood sacrifice was made. It was traditional for the Jews to ritually wash their hands just prior to a meal. In addition to the hand washing *prior* to the meal, immediately *after* the meal, Christ washed the disciples' feet *(John 13:3-5)*, completing the priestly washing of the *hands* and *feet*, and thereby reinforcing to us that we are indeed called to be *priests* unto our God.

Under the new covenant, as new covenant priests,

we are encouraged to attend to such *washings* in the *spirit* by feasting upon God's written word to us and the words He has written on our hearts, allowing them to purge us of our wicked ways. His words are life, and if we meditate on them, they have the power to wash us and realign us to the ways of the kingdom, pushing us toward repentance and the accompanying fruit of *change* that we might be transformed into His image, the image of the only begotten of the Father.

The Lord spiritually washes us by the power of His words to us. We must drink them in and allow them to expose those areas which are inconsistent with the ways of the kingdom that we might loose the speaking power of the blood upon them and turn away from our sin. The water of His word washes us, but it is only the blood of His sacrifice which cleanses us of our unrighteousness; therefore, we must be faithful to appropriate the blood when an area is highlighted by the washing of the water of His words to us. As the Beloved redeemed us with His blood, so He desires to wash us with His words that we might be sanctified unto Him for His good pleasure.

> *...Christ also loved the church and gave Himself for her, that He might sanctify and cleanse her with the washing of water by the word, that He might present her to Himself a glorious church, not having spot or wrinkle or any such thing, but that she should be holy and without blemish.*
>
> *Ephesians 5:25-27*

The water of God's word not only cleanses and purifies our ways, but it *judges* our enemies, proclaiming God's desires to the world around us. By choosing to turn away from our sin and *obey* God's words to us, we are *empowered* to stand against our enemies as did Noah. Noah's *obedience* caused him and his household to enter into God's provision, the ark, that they might not suffer under God's wrath.

By faith Noah, being divinely warned of things not yet seen, moved with godly fear, prepared an ark for the saving of his household, by which he condemned the world and became heir of the righteousness which is according to faith.

Hebrews 11:7

Just as God used water to judge the world in Noah's day after Noah's obedience was complete, so does the water of our Lord's words of life to us today judge the evil within us and around us. *"For the word of God is living and powerful, and sharper than any two-edged sword, piercing even to the division of soul and spirit, and of joints and marrow, and is a discerner of the thoughts and intents of the heart"* (Hebrews 4:12).

His word is indeed a **sword** that is activated at our obedience, *anointing* us to stand against our enemies by faith in God's elaborate provision for us. As we are faithful to proclaim His words and renew our minds by

119

them, we will be transformed and our enemies will be *conquered*, unable to stand under God's judgments.

This is the *water anointing* that prepares us to minister unto our God and stand in judgment against His enemies who have become our enemies. Consecrated unto Him and His purposes, the *dance of the Shulamite* manifests as an expression of our devoted ministry unto the Beloved, releasing His righteous judgments by our own tenacious *obedience* to His words. That is the power of our dance of obedience to Him. It extends the rule of His kingdom, consecrating us as His servants, committed to His purposes.

How can a young man cleanse his way?
By taking heed according to Your word.
With my whole heart I have sought You;
Oh, let me not wander from Your commandments!
Your word I have hidden in my heart,
That I might not sin against You.
Blessed are You, O Lord!
Teach me Your statutes!
With my lips I have declared
All the judgments of Your mouth.
I have rejoiced in the way of Your testimonies,
As much as in all riches.
I will meditate on Your precepts,
And contemplate Your ways.
I will delight myself in Your statutes;

I will not forget Your word.

The Oil Anointing

The *oil anointing* represents the *power* of the Holy Spirit, empowering us with the very fire of God's presence and purging us of defilement as God's fire burns out those things that offend Him.

But who can endure the day of His coming?
And who can stand when He appears?
For He is like a refiner's fire
And like launderers' soap.
He will sit as a refiner and a purifier of silver;
He will purify the sons of Levi,
And purge them as gold and silver,
That they may offer to the Lord
An offering in righteousness.

Malachi 3:2-3

At Pentecost God deposited His Spirit within His people and the manifestation of that was tongues of *fire*. It was a sign of His empowerment of them and His purging of them that they might fulfill their purposes in the kingdom, coming into full fellowship with Him.

As the anointing of the Holy Spirit increases upon our lives, it looses God's judgments upon the earth, declaring His glory; for His judgments are righteous and true, announcing His sovereign rule over the creation. *"A fire goes before Him, and burns up His enemies round about" (Psalm 97:3).* This is one of the jobs of the Holy Spirit, to convict the world of *sin, righteousness, and judgment.*

> *And when He has come, He will convict the world of sin, and of righteousness, and of judgment: of sin, because they do not believe in Me; of righteousness, because I go to My Father and you see Me no more; of judgment, because the ruler of this world is judged.*
> *John 16:8-11*

Since God is a *consuming fire,* His increased presence within His people burns out those things that offend, causing them to manifest His fiery presence to the world and thus prophetically proclaim His ultimate judgment of the earth which will be by fire. *"But the heavens and the earth which are now preserved by the same word, are reserved for fire until the day of judgment and perdition of ungodly men" (2 Peter 3:7).* The earth will be consumed by the fire of His presence and only those who have partaken of His provision for righteousness will stand. *All others will burn.*

> *Let God arise,*
> *Let His enemies be scattered;*
> *Let those also who hate Him flee before Him.*
> *As smoke is driven away,*

So drive them away;
As wax melts before the fire,
So let the wicked perish at the presence of God.
Psalms 68:1-2

Old Testament kings and priests and prophets were all anointed with the oil of anointing because it represented God's call on them, testifying to them that as God had called them to do a job for Him, so He would *empower* them to do it. *The oil represented the anointing of God's very presence upon their lives.* Without this anointing they were powerless, as are we. The Lord reminds us in the scriptures that it is " ... *'Not by might nor by power, but by My Spirit,' Says the Lord of hosts" (Zechariah 4:6b).*

We need His Spirit to abide within us; it is the power of God resident within us to do His good pleasure. *"By this we know that we abide in Him, and He in us, because He has given us of His Spirit" (1 John 4:13).* Yet if we fail to abide in the *blood anointing and the water anointing* which prepare us to house His presence, the Spirit of God will be *grieved* continually, finding no expression in our lives, and we are expressly admonished to *not grieve* the Spirit of the living God *(Ephesians 4:30).*

Therefore, we must be careful to wash in His word and appropriate His blood that His Spirit might be at peace within us; otherwise, the *dance of the Shulamite* will be empowered by soulish zeal. To prevent this defilement, we must submit ourselves daily to the rule of the Holy Spirit in our lives that He might anoint us with the *oil of His presence,* empowering us to truly dance His dance—a *dance of peace* to God and a *dance of war* against His enemies.

The Three Work as One

The three anointings of the water, the blood, and the oil are actually present when we are born into the kingdom of God. Indeed, it is the *Spirit* who draws us through the conviction of God's *word* that we might partake of the *blood* sacrifice of the Son's atonement on the cross. As we grow and mature in the Lord and His ways, these anointings increase in our lives, paving the way for us to fulfill our destinies in the kingdom. In fact, as revelation concerning these three anointings increases, we move from a place of *knowing about the kingdom, to living and abiding in the kingdom,* and that is a place of *empowerment* that we all desire.

These three anointings bear a mystery and can be explored only within the confines of a marriage relationship with the Beloved, Yeshua ha Meshiach. His mysteries truly are hidden and reserved for those who seek them out, delving into the deeper things of God and His ways. *"The secret of the Lord is with those who fear Him, and He will show them His covenant" (Psalm 25:14).*

We as His bride are called to minister unto the Lord as a *priest*; to declare His truth to the world as His *prophet*; and to bring His kingdom to bear on the earth, ruling and reigning with Him as a *king*. To accomplish these tasks we need increased revelation of His *blood anointing* which brings us in past the veil, His *water anointing* which baptizes us into His purposes as obedient servants washed by the water of His word, and His *oil anointing* which is the testimony of His abiding presence within us.

The success of our conquests will directly depend upon the presence and power of these anointings in our lives, for they are expressions of God Himself. That is why it is so important that we subject ourselves to His chastenings, for He desperately desires to increase these anointings within us. Inevitably, such an increase will involve the pruning and cutting away of our flesh which wars against His purposes; yet, if we allow Him to have His way with us, we will bear these anointings, and their fragrance will bear testimony in heaven of our total subjection to the will of the Beloved.

Now thanks be to God who always leads us in triumph in Christ, and through us diffuses the fragrance of His knowledge in every place. For we are to God the fragrance of Christ among those who are being saved and among those who are perishing. To the one we are the aroma of death leading to death, and to the other the aroma of life leading to life. And who is sufficient for these things?

II Corinthians 2:14-16

That is the fragrance He desires to smell—*the fragrance of a life hidden in Him and covered in His provision for godliness.* That is the essence of the mystery and power of His three anointings on the earth—that God could and would dwell in the frailty of man to the glory of God Himself and His creation. That is the basis from which God's kingdom is extended throughout the earth, through submitted lives which are given over to the Beloved for His good pleasure.

Essentially, these anointings are the power and might of God's end-time army, an army of submitted lovers of God, *anointed by God Himself, empowered by God Himself, and clothed by God Himself.* That is His bride, an army of *dancing warriors* covered in ***His blood,*** proclaiming ***His word*** to the world, and walking in the power of ***His Spirit.***

As we grow in revelation of the power of His atonement and die to our own ways, we will find a way to abide in the *authority* of His atonement. Similarly, as we embrace His words to us, choosing to believe them over the lies of the enemy, we will be washed by them and *empowered* by the essence of their message. Interestingly, it was these two "anointings" of the *blood* and the *water* which allowed the old covenant priests to fellowship with the Lord in the Holy Place.

Likewise, it is as we learn to abide in these two "outer court" anointings that we will cease to grieve the Holy Spirit, liberating Him to abide with us in increasing measure, thus enabling us for every task that has been put before us in the kingdom.

May the dance of the Shulamite come forth, for it does indeed bear the fragrance of these anointings, proclaiming His glorious kingdom and ushering in the Beloved's long awaited return. Thus is God's kingdom expressed here on earth as it is in heaven. This is the true heart's cry of the Bride.

> *Your kingdom come.*
> *Your will be done*
> *On earth as it is in heaven.*
> *Matthew 6:10*

XV. THE CONQUEST OF
OUR INHERITANCE

There comes a time when the Beloved beckons us to follow Him into war for our ultimate inheritance in Him. It is then that He leads us out of the wilderness...

Who is this coming up from the wilderness,
Leaning upon her beloved?
I awakened you under the apple tree.
There your mother brought you forth;
There she who bore you brought you forth.
                                    Song 8:5

While sojourning in the wilderness with the Beloved, learning His ways and nurturing a single-eyed devotion for Him, we find ourselves becoming increasingly *dependent* upon Him. Our head comes to rest in surrender and adoration upon His chest with our ear tuned to the *desires of His heart.* We are lovesick and of no use to anyone but Him. It is then that He looses us to do His bidding, commissioning us to take the *land of our inheritance.*

It is at that point that we have entered into His *abiding presence* and that presence anoints us to appear as mighty as He in the spirit realm, for we bear His likeness and the fragrance of His anointings. Though weak and lowly in the physical realm, in the spirit realm the sight of us coming up from the *wilderness* incites awe; for we do indeed appear as an *army with banners*. In fact, we appear just as glorious and intimidating as Solomon's couch surrounded by all of his mighty men.

Who is this coming out of the wilderness
Like pillars of smoke,
Perfumed with myrrh and frankincense,
With all the merchant's fragrant powders?
Behold, it is Solomon's couch,
With sixty valiant men around it,
Of the valiant of Israel.
They all hold swords,
Being expert in war.
Every man has his sword on his thigh
Because of fear in the night.
                                    Song 3:6-8

It is this sight that testifies to the spirit realm that we have become useful to the Master as a lover who faithfully does His bidding with joy. It is then that our transformation into God's formidable army causes us to be sent out for the purposes of *conquest and war*. It is out of such submitted devotion that God commissions us as warriors who will chase our enemies by the sword.

This is the final stage of our warfare for His kingdom. Previously, we warred against our *own strongholds* that kept us back from our inheritance. Now it is time to extend the kingdom of God beyond our families and friends. This type of warfare will involve a dispossession of enemy territory through our consistent habitation of the "land" of *His presence,* seated with Him in heavenly places.

As our Lord allowed us to be tested repeatedly in the wilderness, it can now be said of us that *the enemy has no part in us,* just as it was said of Him after His wilderness experience. We are the Beloved's, and thus *His habitation and His inheritance.* As such, we are an intimidating force which the enemy cannot stand against, for our Messiah now has full expression in us and through us.

> *I will set My tabernacle among you, and My soul shall not abhor you.*
> *I will walk among you and be your God, and you shall be My people.*
> *I am the Lord your God, who brought you out of the land of Egypt, that you should not be their slaves;*
> *I have broken the bands of your yoke and made you walk upright.*
>
> *Leviticus 26:11-13*

Not all who come to salvation will hear this call to serve in the Beloved's great army. Only those who have been clothed in His special *wedding garments* will hear this call to war. In fact, it is our *wedding garments* which will gird us up for such warfare, distinguishing us as those who have entered into *intimacy* with the Son, taking on the power and authority of *His righteousness*. Consequently, without such garments of intimacy, we will surely be excluded from service in this great army of overcomers, as well as from the great wedding feast to come.

But when the king came in to see the guests, he saw a man there who did not have on a wedding garment. So he said to him, "Friend, how did you come in here without a wedding garment?" And he was speechless. Then the king said to the servants, "Bind him hand and foot, take him away, and cast him into outer darkness; there will be weeping and gnashing of teeth." For many are called, but few are chosen.
Matthew 22:11-14

In this parable about the wedding feast, one of the guests was thrown out of the brilliance of the Lord's inner chambers to a place of *darkness*, where those who see what they have missed out on weep and gnash their teeth. *"But the sons of the kingdom will be cast out into outer darkness. There will be weeping and gnashing of teeth" (Matthew 8:12).*

The Lord has many who follow Him whom He

calls *concubines, queens, and virgins.* These are those who have entered in through the door of *salvation* but have turned away from the door of *intimacy.* However, the Beloved's chaste bride, *His dove,* is the *only one* birthed into intimacy with Him through the ministry of His Holy Spirit. She is made up of those who have said *yes* to Him, for as He told us, *"Many are called, but few are chosen,"* and it is *we* who choose how close we will come to Him. Though He extends this glorious invitation to *all,* only a few say *yes.* They are the ones He calls *His dove, His only one.*

Like a piece of pomegranate
Are your temples behind your veil.
There are sixty queens
And eighty concubines,
And virgins without number.
My dove, my perfect one,
Is the only one,
The only one of her mother,
The favorite of the one who bore her.
The daughters saw her
And called her blessed,
The queens and the concubines,
And they praised her.
Who is she who looks forth as the morning,
Fair as the moon,
Clear as the sun,
Awesome as an army with banners?

Song 6:7-10

This is the Beloved's description of His bride, *His dove, His only one*, veiled by His own attentions and beholding Him with *dove's eyes*. It is our single-eyed devotion which will cause us to be joined to His purposes, transforming us into warring *"chariots,"* the chariots of a *noble people*, God's people.

> *I went down to the garden of nuts*
> *To see the verdure of the valley,*
> *To see whether the vine had budded*
> *And the pomegranates had bloomed.*
> *Before I was even aware,*
> *My soul had made me*
> *As the chariots of my noble people.*
> *Song 6:11-12*

It is the Bride's intimate sojourn through the *"garden of nuts"* that will cause this great transformation. As she faithfully watches the times and seasons of this special *garden* of the kingdom, she will be joined to the heartbeat of the Groom, and His desires will become her desires, transforming her into mighty *"chariots"* of war for the purposes of His kingdom. It is the roar of these *"chariots"* that will incite fear into God's enemies, actually *draining their faces of color.*

> *With a noise like chariots*
> *Over mountain tops they leap,*
> *Like the noise of a flaming fire that devours*
> *the stubble,*

Like a strong people set in battle array.
Before them the people writhe in pain;
All faces are drained of color.

Joel 2:5-6

This is the ultimate *dance of war* expressed by the Bride—*the conquest of her inheritance.* Our conquest in His name is actually an expression of His judgment in the earth. When He leads us out to war, we are so full of the fire of His abiding presence that we are a *consuming fire* that devours His enemies. *"A fire devours before them, and behind them a flame burns... (Joel 2:3a).* That is the fervor of the *Shulamite's dance of war.* It is a dance fervently fueled by God Himself and not our own arduous zealotry. It is fueled by His passion for us and our passion for Him, causing us to be in complete *subjection to His desires.* Thus will the Shulamite's prophetic proclamation concerning the Bride of Yeshua come to fullness; *"I am my beloved's, and His desire is toward me" (Song 7:10).*

It is the manifestation of this truth which testifies that the Beloved's avid training of us has utterly eradicated our defiling agendas and grievous carnality from our midst. Thus is it unquestionably apparent that the Beloved has caused His bride to take on *His ways,* becoming one with His purposes in the earth. *"For we are members of His body, of His flesh and of His bones" (Ephesians 5:30).* This is the mystery of Messiah Yeshua becoming one with the Church, His bride. He is the head, and she is His body.

> *And Adam said:*
> *"This is now bone of my bones*
> *And flesh of my flesh;*
> *She shall be called Woman,*
> *Because she was taken out of Man."*
> *Genesis 2:23*

As woman was birthed of the first Adam and became one with his flesh, so the Beloved's Bride has been birthed out of the second Adam, Yeshua ha Meshiach, and is destined to become *one flesh* with Him, joined to His purposes. As His namesake on the earth, walking in the fullness of the authority of that name which is above every other name, we are called to further His kingdom and lay claim to the land of our inheritance for His name's sake. That land involves the expression of our callings and purposes in the kingdom of God that have been hidden within us before the foundation of the world. The claiming of this land and the occupying of it is the *pinnacle* of our unique dance of devotion to the Beloved. It is our own *dance of the Shulamite,* and it is ultimately manifested out of *conquest,* a conquest into which He leads us.

We as His bride have been chosen to war by His side and bring the kingdom of God to earth, ruling and reigning with Him. We have been chosen to bear His name and extend His authority throughout the earth. We are His expression on the earth. We are His inheritance and He is ours.

> *In Him also we have obtained an inheritance,*
> *being predestined according to the purpose of*
> *Him who works all things according to the*
> *counsel of His will, that we who first trusted*
> *in Christ should be to the praise of His glory...*
> *And He put all things under His feet, and gave*
> *Him to be head over all things to the church,*
> *which is His body, the fullness of Him who fills*
> *all in all.*
>
> *Ephesians 1:11-12; 22-23*

XVI. THE DANCE OF THE OVERCOMING BRIDE

The Beloved's bride is destined to become an army of overcomers who have made themselves ready by subjecting themselves to Yeshua ha Meshiach and His ways, arrayed in His righteousness and executing mighty acts of faith in His name.

This is the Dance of the Shulamite for the Beloved!

And to her it was granted to be arrayed in fine linen, clean and bright, for the fine linen is the righteous acts of the saints.

Revelation 19:8

This army of *dancing lovesick warriors* will be known for its single-eyed devotion to the Groom. Because of their total dependence upon Him, they will have no need to make their own way, jostling for position through self-promotion and manipulation. They will have found their ordained position within His body—*the position for which they were created.* Consequently, their lives will be unique and wondrous expressions of their call to serve the Beloved.

The spiritual playing out of these callings and purposes in the kingdom will appear as beautiful choreographed dances, full of creative life and breathtaking motion that emulate and glorify the Creator. They will constitute the great *Dance of the Shulamite.*

This is the dance of all dances, and it is the dance that will so enthrall the Groom, Yeshua ha Meshiach, that He will literally be overcome by its intrinsic majesty and grace. It will be a dance which portrays the unique beauty and glorious splendor of the kingdom within all of us, a beauty and splendor which was deposited in each of us before the foundation of the world.

> *O my love, you are as beautiful as Tirzah,*
> *Lovely as Jerusalem,*
> *Awesome as an army with banners!*
> *Turn your eyes away from me,*
> *For they have overcome me.*
> *Your hair is like a flock of goats*
> *Going down from Gilead.*
>
> Song 6:4-5

This is a dance which will fulfill our divinely

appointed purposes in the kingdom. Those purposes essentially involve our priestly worship and adoration of the Beloved, our proclamation of His kingdom to all the earth, and the subjugation of the powers of darkness to our Beloved's rule out of our own decided obedience. What a glorious dance this is! *It is a dance of devotion and a dance of conquest. It is a dance of love and a dance of war.* **It is the Dance of the Shulamite for the Beloved.** It is the dance for which the whole creation is groaning in anticipation, as it is the fullness of the kingdom come to earth.

For the earnest expectation of the creation eagerly waits for the revealing of the sons of God. For the creation was subjected to futility, not willingly, but because of Him who subjected it in hope; because the creation itself also will be delivered from the bondage of corruption into the glorious liberty of the children of God. For we know that the whole creation groans and labors with birth pangs together until now.

Romans 8:19-22

Joel saw a picture of this marvelous dance of devotion for which the creation *groans.* In a vision of God's mighty end-time army, he described each member as marching in his or her assigned column, dutifully fulfilling his or her ordained commission, moving gracefully in and out of enemy territory, accomplishing exploits for the kingdom.

141

They run like mighty men,
They climb the wall like men of war;
Every one marches in formation,
And they do not break ranks.
They do not push one another;
Every one marches in his own column.
Though they lunge between the weapons,
They are not cut down.
They run to and fro in the city,
They run on the wall;
They climb into the houses,
They enter at the windows like a thief.
The earth quakes before them,
The heavens tremble;
The sun and moon grow dark,
And the stars diminish their brightness.
The Lord gives voice before His army,
For His camp is very great;
For strong is the One who executes His word.
For the day of the Lord is great and very terrible;
Who can endure it?

Joel 2:7-11

This army of overcomers will be groomed and trained in the *wilderness of His preparation*. As such, it is imperative that we set our eyes on the Beloved, allowing Him to teach us the dance steps of the kingdom, decidedly turning away from our other dances and choosing to dance the dance of death that has been specially choreographed for each of us that we might dance this unique and wondrous dance of life, the ***Dance of the Shulamite for the Beloved.***

May we all have dove's eyes behind the *veil*, the veil that hides us from the world until the day when the Bride has made herself ready and is gloriously unveiled for all the creation to behold her beauty, the beauty of the prophetic manifestation of the *sons of God*. Therefore, do the *daughters* and the *friends* of the Beloved beckon the *Shulamite* to return to her prophetic *promised land* that her beauty might come to fullness for all to behold.

> *Return, return, O Shulamite;*
> *Return, return, that we may look upon you!*
> *What would you see in the Shulamite—*
> *As it were, the dance of the two camps?*
> *Song 6:13*

This is the manifestation that the creation groans for—*the glory of the Bride,* a glory that will be admired even by those who have chosen not to enter through the door of intimacy. It is the beauty of Yeshua's manifest presence upon His chosen ones, those who have been hidden away in His chambers, feasting upon Him for their very sustenance, causing them to obey His every desire as *worshiping lovesick warriors.*

This intimate *Dance of the Shulamite* will be

prophetically danced by *two camps* of people, Jew and Gentile, who will be united into one bride. It should be noted that the phrase, *"the two camps,"* is translated from the Hebrew word, *"Mahanaim."* This was the name Jacob gave to the place where the angels met him on his return to Canaan prior to meeting with his brother, Esau. Jacob perceived that the place he was in was indeed the camp of the Lord. *"So Jacob went on his way, and the angels of God met him. When Jacob saw them, he said, 'This is God's camp.' And he called the name of the place Mahanaim"* (Genesis 32:1-2).

Interestingly, Jacob returned to his homeland with *two* wives and eleven sons, and as he prepared to meet Esau, he divided his people into *two camps*, representing the prophetic return of God's bride to Zion, the place of God's habitation.

As Yeshua's bride gains a deeper revelation of who she is in Him, she too will spiritually return to her *promised land*, returning to her Hebraic roots as God's *chosen people*, comprised of *two camps*, Jew and Gentile. Even now, God is whistling for His bride. Some are being called to *physically* return to the promised land of Israel, while *all* are being called out of the carnality of mere religion to return to their *spiritual* promised land in Him, finding a place of habitation and abundant life in *spiritual Zion* where He resides.

For I will set My eyes on them for good, and I will

bring them back to this land; I will build them and not pull them down, and I will plant them and not pluck them up.

Then I will give them a heart to know Me, that I am the Lord; and they shall be My people, and I will be their God for they shall return to Me with their whole heart.

Jeremiah 24:6-7

The Beloved first betrothed Himself to His bride at Mt. Sinai, after delivering His people from Egypt, and when He came to earth the first time it was as the great Kinsman-Redeemer that He might purchase His bride with His own blood. Now through the ministry of His Holy Spirit, He is gathering His bride to Himself by writing His *law* upon their hearts and calling them out of *Babylon*. Thus, will the Beloved's second appearing on earth be for the purposes of consummating this mysterious marriage and dwelling with His bride, *His inheritance in the earth.*

This bride for whom God is whistling is prophetically characterized in the scriptures as *Ephraim* and *Judah*. Ephraim was the dominant of the ten northern tribes of Israel, and therefore its name is used to designate these ten rebellious tribes who turned from God's ways and chose to serve God as every man thought in his own heart and not as God had directed in His word. Ending up in exile, these assimilated Jews became a physical representation of a wayward

Ephraim, sown into the nations. A prophetic picture of Ephraim's assimilation is notably evidenced in much of the Gentile Church which has turned away from its Hebraic roots and whored after the ways of the world, becoming an assimilated people as well. *Judah*, on the other hand, is pictured by the Jewish people who have guarded God's law in their hearts, but have been blinded to the revelation of Yeshua ha Meshiach. In these two camps of people do we see the picture of the parable of the Prodigal Son, for it is the return of *Ephraim*, the prodigal, to a pure devotion for the Beloved which will ultimately move *Judah* to jealousy, removing the veil and causing both camps to be unified in passion and purpose as the "called out ones," the *Bride of Yeshua.* Zechariah saw this mystifying "union" of the two camps and prophesied of it.

I will strengthen the house of Judah,
And I will save the house of Joseph.
I will bring them back,
Because I have mercy on them.
They shall be as though I had not cast them aside;
For I am the Lord their God,
And I will hear them.
Those of Ephraim shall be like a mighty man,
And their heart shall rejoice as if with wine.
Yes, their children shall see it and be glad;
Their heart shall rejoice in the Lord,
I will whistle for them and gather them,
For I will redeem them;

And they shall increase as they once increased.
I will sow them among the peoples,
And they shall remember Me in far countries;
They shall live, together with their children,
And they shall return.
I will also bring them back from the land of Egypt.
And gather them from Assyria.
I will bring them into the land of Gilead and
*   Lebanon,*
Until no more room is found for them.

Zechariah 10:6-10

The prophetic destiny of *Judah* and *Ephraim* was significantly portrayed when the children of Israel made their conquest of the promised land, led by the faithful report of Caleb, of the tribe of *Judah*, and Joshua, of the tribe of *Ephraim*. These tribes will again be prophetically represented as the Bride ascends to take the *land* of her spiritual inheritance in Him who is the fullness of all things. When the prophetic camps of *Ephraim* and *Judah* are united according to God's purposes, then will they become *one stick* in the Beloved's mighty hand. The prophet Ezekiel had a revelation of this wondrous *"stick"* that would be God's mighty end-time army of overcomers, His bride, His mighty weapon of war for the last hour.

Thus says the Lord God: "Surely I will take the stick
of Joseph, which is in the hand of Ephraim, and the
tribes of Israel, his companions; and I will join them

with it, with the stick of Judah, and make them one stick, and they will be one in My hand."

And the sticks on which you write will be in your hand before their eyes.

Then say to them, "Thus says the Lord God: 'Surely I will take the children of Israel from among the nations, wherever they have gone, and will gather them from every side and bring them into their own land;

'and I will make them one nation in the land, on the mountains of Israel; and one king shall be king over them all; they shall no longer be two nations, nor shall they ever be divided into two kingdoms again.

'They shall not defile themselves anymore with their idols, nor with their detestable things, nor with any of their transgressions; but I will deliver them from all their dwelling places in which they have sinned, and will cleanse them. Then they shall be My people, and I will be their God.' "

Ezekiel 37:19-23

This mystery of the *one stick* will bear the prophetic significance of the completion represented in Jacob's twelfth son, Benjamin. Just as Benjamin was born *after* Jacob's return to the promised land, so will the return of God's people to the land of their inheritance usher in the birthing of the "one new man," *the manifest sons of God* who will walk in the lavish provision of Benjamin's portion—a five times portion of grace and power, representing the fullness of the five-fold ministry.

This prophetic picture depicted in Benjamin can also be seen in the Apostle Paul's prophetic life and ministry. In the natural, Paul was a Jew of the tribe of Benjamin who possessed Roman citizenship living as a dispersed Jew in Tarsus. Since the tribe of Benjamin remained loyal to the tribe of Judah after the split of the northern tribes from the southern tribes, Paul's ministry pictures a joining of *Judah* (his inheritance in the tribe of Benjamin) and *Ephraim* (his Roman citizenship and ministry to the Gentiles and fellow dispersed Jews) as that "one stick" ministry of fullness. Though born a Roman citizen and raised in a Hellenized city, Paul retained his Jewish roots; and after gaining a revelation of Messiah Yeshua, he shared it with Jew and Gentile. This is the might and power of "Benjamin's portion" flowing from *Judah* and *Ephraim's reunification*–a ministry of reconciliation between Jew and Gentile in Messiah.

The end-time ministry of the Church will truly walk in the many revelations that Paul had of the Church, including the understanding that there is **no** distinction between Jew and Gentile hidden in Messiah. The sons of the kingdom are actually **all** sons of Abraham, sons of faith; united in purpose as one people, a people who will become "one stick" in our Lord's hand. These are the ones for whom the Lord is whistling to return to the land of their inheritance in *Him.*

This great gathering of God's people is happening in the *natural* and in the *spirit.* To be a part of His bride, *all* will have to make the *spiritual journey* to Zion, the place of His habitation, and some will actually be required to return to natural Israel as a prophetic picture of this "habitation." This great spiritual gathering of oneness in Him will become the *habitation of the Lord,* for it is His bride who is *His inheritance.* She is His place of rest, His peace; and He is the Bride's place of rest, her Prince of Peace, her *shalom.* Thus, will a *covenant of peace* seal this great marriage of the ages.

> *Moreover I will make a covenant of peace with them, and it shall be an everlasting covenant with them; I will establish them and multiply them, and I will set My sanctuary in their midst forevermore.*
>
> *My tabernacle also shall be with them; indeed I will be their God, and they shall be My people.*
>
> *The nations also will know that I, the Lord, sanctify Israel, when My sanctuary is in their midst forevermore.*
>
> *Ezekiel 37:26-28*

The Bride will be a *city* for His habitation, a city without walls, for the Lord Himself will be the *wall* that protects His people. " *'For I,' says the Lord, 'will be a wall of fire all around her, and I will be the glory in her midst'* " *(Zechariah 2:5).* This image of Jerusalem is a glorious picture of God dwelling in His inheritance, His bride. She will be a *new Jerusalem,* a place of *peace,* for the Bride will abide in the Beloved and He in her. They will be one another's inheritance as Bride and Bridegroom in the kingdom of our God.

> *"Sing and rejoice, O daughter of Zion! For behold, I am coming and I will dwell in your midst," says the Lord.*

> *"Many nations shall be joined to the Lord in that day, and they shall become My people. And I will dwell in your midst. Then you will know that the Lord of hosts has sent Me to you.*

> *"And the Lord will take possession of Judah as His inheritance in the Holy Land, and will again choose Jerusalem.*

> *"Be silent, all flesh, before the Lord, for He is aroused from His holy habitation!"*
>
> *Zechariah 2:10-13*

This is the glory of the Bride which will capture the heart of the Beloved and astonish the eyes of the world, causing the ungodly to either repent or gnash their teeth in offense at her *righteousness* which will actually be *His righteousness*. When the Bride has entered into such a *habitation* of pure devotion and abandoned obedience to the Son, then will her heart's cry truly join with that of the Spirit of the living God, ushering in the long anticipated return of the Groom for His glorious bride. She will indeed long for the Beloved as much as He longs for her, causing the kingdom to resound with the prophetic longing of the Bride and the Spirit crying out in unison for His majestic return.

And the Spirit and the bride say, "Come!"
And let him who hears say, "Come!"

And let him who thirsts come.
Whoever desires, let him take the water of life freely.
Revelation 22:17

This is the moment the creation awaits, when the Bride and the Bridegroom are united in purpose and desire at the great *wedding feast of the Lamb* as God joins Himself to His people that they might rule and reign together as one. This is the heartbeat of God's passion for His creation, that His bride would be by His side, accomplishing His purposes with Him.

And I heard, as it were, the voice of a great multitude,
as the sound of many waters and as the sound of

mighty thunderings, saying "Alleluia! For the Lord
God Omnipotent reigns!

"Let us be glad and rejoice and give Him glory, for
the marriage of the Lamb has come, and His wife has
made herself ready."

And to her it was granted to be arrayed in fine linen,
clean and bright, for the fine linen is the righteous
acts of the saints.

Then he said to me, "Write: 'Blessed are those who
are called to the marriage supper of the Lamb!' "
                                                    Revelation 19:6-9

May we all be invited to this great wedding feast of
the ages. It is an invitation reserved only for those who
have counted the cost, choosing *to follow the Lamb*
wherever He leads, loving not their lives to the death.
It is these whom Joel saw as the formidable *army of*
God, those who will fight by the Lamb's side in the last
great war, executing His judgments in the earth
alongside Him; and it is these whom John saw as the
armies of heaven, accompanying our Lord in His return
for vengeance. These are those who have danced *a*
dance of unbridled passion for the Son of God,
expressed in extravagant acts of obedience. This is the
great and magnificent Bride of Yeshua who will woo
the Beloved to return for her—His Shulamite lover,
His dove, His only one.

Now I saw heaven opened, and behold, a white horse. And He who sat on him was called Faithful and True, and in righteousness He judges and makes war. His eyes were like a flame of fire, and on His head were many crowns. He had a name written that no one knew except Himself. He was clothed with a robe dipped in blood, and His name is called The Word of God. And the armies in heaven, clothed in fine linen, white and clean, followed Him on white horses. Now out of His mouth goes a sharp sword, that with it He should strike the nations. And He Himself will rule them with a rod of iron. He Himself treads the winepress of the fierceness and wrath of Almighty God. And He has on His robe and on His thigh a name written:

KING OF KINGS
AND LORD OF LORDS.

Revelation 19:11-16

A Final Encouragement
in Your Quest for Holy Passion

It must be reiterated that such divine passion for the Son must be activated by His own personal attentions to us—that divine *glance* which enraptures us. If we try to emulate this type of passion, we will die in the arduous task of attempting to fuel such love through vain self-righteous acts of piety; for love of this kind has a price tag, which *only* the Beloved can pay. *"For you were bought at a price; therefore glorify God in your body and in your spirit, which are God's" (I Corinthians 6:20).*

As one who has felt *His glorious left hand under my head and His strong right hand embracing me,* I urge you to allow the Beloved the freedom to mature His love in you. He is faithful to raise up the love He desires from His bride.

If you truly desire to dance the dance of all dances unto the Beloved, permit Him to gently lead you to His special garden where His *apple tree of intimacy* is found, the place were love is awakened and holy passion for the Son is miraculously ignited. It is then that His mark of ownership will be upon you, causing Him to jealously hide you out in the *wilderness of His choosing*, preparing you for your kingdom purposes as *a conqueror*; for we are truly called to *rule and reign* with Him as His glorious bride, dancing the dance of the ages, the great *Dance of the Shulamite for the Beloved, Yeshua ha Meshiach.*

His left hand is under my head,
And his right hand embraces me.
I charge you, O daughters of Jerusalem,
Do not stir up nor awaken love
Until it pleases.

Who is this coming up from the wilderness,
Leaning upon her beloved?
I awakened you under the apple tree.
There your mother brought you forth;
There she who bore you brought you forth.

Set me as a seal upon your heart,
As a seal upon your arm;
For love is as strong as death,
Jealousy as cruel as the grave;
Its flames are flames of fire,
A most vehement flame.

Many waters cannot quench love,
Nor can the floods drown it.
If a man would give for love
All the wealth of his house,
It would be utterly despised.

                                                Song 8:3-7

About the Author...

Barbara Urban has ministered overseas in women's conferences, interceded at onsite locations, and prayed for the sick and demon possessed. Her ministry, *Shulamite Creations*, is dedicated to instilling a passion for intimacy with the Beloved in those with ears to hear. The Lord specifically uses Barbara to host Feasts of the Lord, inviting God's people to peer into the secrets of the inner courts of God's presence, leading them in prophetic experiences which are full of kingdom pictures concerning our life in Messiah. Using our Hebraic roots, she unfolds the richness of Yeshua's blood which ever speaks on our behalf and the full provision that has been made for us to hear and obey our Lord's voice within the context of an intimate love relationship with Him.

Barbara is committed to educating Jew and Gentile about who the true Israel of God is and how our prophetic intercession for natural Israel will help to unfold the mystery of a *united Israel* who will be an empowered, overcoming bride, abiding in Him – *the land of her inheritance.*

For further information about *Shulamite Creations*, you may contact Barbara by e-mail.

Shulamite@mindspring.com

Impac Chris ian Books

332 Leffingwell Ave., Suite 101
Kirkwood, MO 63122

AVAILABLE AT YOUR LOCAL BOOKSTORE, OR YOU MAY ORDER DIRECTLY. Toll-Free, order-line only M/C, DISC, or VISA 1-800-451-2708.

Visit our Website at *www. impactchristianbooks.com*

Write for *FREE* Catalog.